REFERENCE

D0496805

The Forward book of poetry
2008

The Forward book of poetry
2008

WITHDRAWN

FORWARD

LONDON

COTTISH POETRY LIF
By leaves w·
5 Crichton's Close
Edinburgh
EH8 8DT
Tel 0131 557 28

First published in Great Britain by
Forward Ltd · 84–86 Regent Street · London W1B 5DD
in association with
Faber and Faber · 3 Queen Square · London WC1N 3AU

ISBN 978 0 571 23957 3 (paperback)

Compilation copyright © Forward Ltd 2007
Foreword copyright © Michael Symmons Roberts

Reprographics by Zebra
Printed by Antony Rowe Ltd
Bumper's Farm · Chippenham · Wiltshire SN14 6LH · UK

All rights reserved. Without limiting the rights under copyright
reserved, no part of this publication may be reproduced,
stored in or introduced into a retrieval system or transmitted, in any
form or by any means (electronic, mechanical, photocopying,
recording or otherwise), without the prior written permission of both
the copyright owner and the above publisher of this book.

A CIP catalogue reference for this book
is available at the British Library.

35133
C 30·10·07

To Philip Wells with love

Preface

THE NEWS THAT, among this year's nominees for the Forward Prize, was the former political prisoner and human rights activist Jack Mapanje, who spent three years imprisoned without charge in his home country of Malawi, perhaps inevitably garnered a good deal of media attention – as well it might. Freedom is a basic human right, but it seems to me that it is also at the heart of all good poetry, whatever the circumstances of its creation. Not just the freedom to say what one thinks, but in a wider sense too: freedom to experiment, freedom to think outside the common language of the everyday, even the freedom to test the boundaries of logic and understanding. Poetry, it has sometimes been said, is play, but it can also be deadly serious; after all, it was a book of poetry that got Jack Mapanje thrown in jail in the first place. So let us celebrate his freedom, but let us celebrate the freedom of poetry too: we would all be diminished without it.

Reading this year's anthology has been a pleasure made keener by the knowledge that the judges – led this year by Michael Symmons Roberts, with Jean 'Binta' Breeze, Sarah Crown, Colin Greenwood and Glyn Maxwell – have already done most of the hard work by choosing from an entire year's worth of published poetry. My sincere thanks to them for their hard work and dedication, which deserves a verse or two of its own.

The Forward Prize could not continue without the sterling support of our many partners: the inestimable Felix Dennis; Jules Mann and The Poetry Society; John Hampson and Arts Council England; Faber and Faber; the Colman Getty team, including Dotti Irving, Liz Sich, Kate Wright-Morris and Truda Spruyt; and everyone at Forward.

William Sieghart

Foreword

EVERYONE SAYS IT'S TOUGH TO JUDGE A BOOK PRIZE, but there's tough and *tough*. The hardest part of the Forward judging comes with the exclusions, the need to cut the shortlists back and set aside books of fine writing in order to settle on a final few. But this painful process is only half the story. The real pleasure is in the reading, and this anthology reflects the passions and preoccupations of the judges after reading 120 books.

There's a piece of jargon in film-making – popular in documentary television just now – that describes successful films as 'an immersive experience'. It struck me as an annoying and empty phrase, but I found it coming back to me this summer. It's something to do with the range and depth of the Forward Prizes. In a few short weeks you lose yourself in the best recent work by established poets, the best new blood brought forward by the growing number of poetry presses and publishers, and the most striking single poems nominated by the magazines that published them.

I read a lot of poetry at the best (and worst) of times – as do all this year's judges – but I don't normally indulge in what my fellow judge Sarah Crown described as a 'great poetry binge'. In her *Guardian* blog Sarah said she felt changed by a summer spent reading nothing but poems. By the end of it she was reading with greater focus, perception and attention. She also described as a 'rare privilege' the opportunity to take in a year's worth of published poetry in a few weeks.

We all noticed through our reading that certain themes (even particular words) kept surfacing. In particular this year *water* was a key theme in individual poems and whole collections. It's tempting to ascribe this preoccupation to our summer deluge, but all these books were written well before the floods. Is this proof of the collective unconscious? Does poetry have prophetic power? Is life – or the weather at least – imitating art? Take your pick. Whatever the explanation, this year's poetry is drenched.

When all the reading gave way to the talking, the strength and breadth of this year's haul of books was reflected in the wide range of choices each of the judges brought to the table. In the end, the shortlisted books and poems in each category had to win the support of all the judges, and although (inevitably) each of us could list several more books we would love to have included, we all feel that the shortlists are strong, varied, and full of remarkable writing.

Of course, the Forward process isn't just about the shortlists. Each of us had half an eye on this anthology as we worked our way through the boxes of books. All of the poems in this book were discussed and chosen at the shortlisting meeting. It gave us a chance to honour books that would have made a longer list. It also allowed us to recognise some astonishing single poems from books we felt were more mixed, or books that inspired love in one or other of us, and indifference in the rest. In short, this book is a snapshot of this year's poetry, or rather this year's poetry as seen by these five judges in a summer of 'immersive' reading.

It has been a great pleasure to talk poetry with my fellow judges Glyn Maxwell, Sarah Crown, Jean 'Binta' Breeze and Colin Greenwood. At the moment of writing this, the winners in each category are yet to be decided, and I look forward to our final discussions in October, though not without some trepidation.

As ever, the Forward Prizes are dependent on the vision and generosity of their founder, William Sieghart, and the patience, persistence and sheer organisational genius of Kate Wright-Morris. I hope this anthology will serve as a celebration of the health and strength of this year's poetry.

Michael Symmons Roberts, July 2007

Publisher acknowledgements

Louise Adjoa Parker · Rag Doll · *Salt-sweat & Tears* · Cinnamon Press

Tiffany Atkinson · Zuppa di Ceci · *Kink and Particle* · Seren

John Barnie · Easter 3000 · *Trouble in Heaven* · Gomer Press

Suzanne Batty · Shrink · *The Barking Thing* · Bloodaxe Books

Nazand Begikhani · An Ordinary Day · *Bells of Speech* · Ambit

Eavan Boland · How it Was Once in Our Country · Inheritance · *Domestic Violence* · Carcanet Press

Joanna Boulter · Fugue · Prelude · *Twenty Four Preludes and Fugues on Dimitri Shostakovich* · Arc Publications

John Burnside · By Pittenweem · *Gift Songs* · Jonathan Cape

Anne Carson · Walks for Girls and Boys · London Review of Books

James Caruth · This Man · *A Stone's Throw* · Staple Press

Ian Caws · Apple Day · Ambit

Melanie Challenger · *from* The Service of the Heart and The Spark of Transgression · *Galatea* · Salt Publishing

Jennifer Copley · Ten Places Where I See My Mother · *Unsafe Monuments* · Arrowhead Press

Nick Drake · c/o the Sea at Patea · *From the Word Go* · Bloodaxe Books

Sasha Dugdale · Song of a Wanderer · *The Estate* · Oxford Poets (Carcanet Press)

Ian Duhig · Fauvel Love Song · *The Speed of Dark* · Picador

Helen Dunmore · To My Nine-Year-Old Self · *Glad of These Times* · Bloodaxe Books

Kate Edwards · Parallel Universes · The Journal

Elaine Feinstein · London · *Talking to the Dead* · Carcanet Press

Annie Freud · The Manipulation of Words · *The Best Man There Ever Was* · Picador

Cynthia Fuller · They Said · *Jack's Letters Home* · Flambard Press

John Fuller · The Meditation · The Future · *The Space of Joy* · Chatto & Windus

Tess Gallagher · Black Beauty · *Dear Ghosts,* · Bloodaxe Books

John Goodby · The Uncles · Cardiff International Poetry Competition

Dana Goodyear · County Line Road · *Honey and Junk* · WW Norton & Company

Ann Gray · Your body · The Shop: A Magazine of Poetry

David Harsent · THE HUT IN QUESTION · Poetry Review
Geoffrey Hill · CITATIONS I · *A Treatise of Civil Power* · Penguin Books
Jane Hirshfield · SKY: AN ASSAY · *After* · Bloodaxe Books
Judy Kendall · UNDETERRED · *The Drier the Brighter* · Cinnamon Press
Luke Kennard · THE JOURNALIST'S PRAYER · THE MURDERER · *The Harbour Beyond the Movie* · Salt Publishing
Nick Laird · USE OF SPIES · *On Purpose* · Faber and Faber
Jenny Lewis · INANA · *Fathom* · Oxford Poets (Carcanet Press)
Tim Liardet · *from* NORTH OF EVERYTHING · Poetry Review
Joanne Limburg · THE FALL · *Paraphernelia* · Bloodaxe Books
John McAuliffe · TOWN · *Next Door* · Gallery Books
Mary MacRae · JURY · Orbis
Allison McVety · PORTRAIT · Poetry News
Sarah Maguire · THE WATER DIVINER · *The Pomegranates of Kandahar* · Chatto & Windus
Jack Mapanje · THE SEASHELLS OF BRIDLINGTON NORTH BEACH · THE WEDDING OF JACARANDAS · *Beasts of Nalunga* · Bloodaxe Books
Lorraine Mariner · THURSDAY · The Rialto
Kathy Miles · A LONDON TALE · The Interpreter's House
David Morley · FICTION · *The Invisible Kings* · Carcanet Press
Sharon Morris · FOR THE FIG TREE · *False Spring* · Enitharmon Press
Graham Mort · ADVERTISING EXECUTIVE WITH SPARROWHAWK · *Visibility* · Seren
Paul Muldoon · SOCCER MOMS · *Horse Latitudes* · Faber and Faber
Daljit Nagra · DARLING & ME! · A PRELUDE TO SUKA'S ADVENTURES FROM THE BOARD ROOM · *Look We Have Coming to Dover!* · Faber and Faber
Sean O'Brien · DRAINS · THE BRAZIER · *The Drowned Book* · Picador
Michael O'Siadhail · SKEINS · *Globe* · Bloodaxe Books
Alice Oswald · DUNT · Poetry London
Marita Over · SPIDERS · *Not Knowing Itself* · Arrowhead Press
Sandeep Parmar · THE OCTAGONAL TOWER · The Wolf
Mario Petrucci · NIGHT FLAW · *Flowers of Sulphur* · Enitharmon Press
Jacob Polley · THE OWLS · *Little Gods* · Picador
Eleanor Rees · NIGHT VISION · ANDRASTE'S HAIR · *Andraste's Hair* · Salt Publishing
Maurice Riordan · *from* THE IDYLLS · *The Holy Land* · Faber and Faber
Neil Rollinson · WILDLIFE · *Demolition* · Jonathan Cape

Contents

Highly Commended Poems 2007

Shortlisted Poems
The Forward Prize for Best Collection

Eavan Boland

How it Was Once in Our Country

In those years I owned a blue plate,
blue from the very edges to the centre,
ocean-blue, the sort of under-wave blue
a mermaid could easily dive down into and enter.

When I looked at the plate I saw the mouth
of a harbour, an afternoon without a breath
of air, the evening clear all the way to Howth
and back, the sky a paler blue further to the south.

Consider the kind of body that enters blueness,
made out of dead-end myth and mischievous
whispers of an old, borderless
existence where the body's meaning is both more and less.

Sea-trawler, land-siren: succubus to all the dreams
land has of ocean, of its old home.
She must have witnessed deaths. Of course she did.
Some say she stayed down there to escape the screams.

INHERITANCE

I have been wondering
what I have to leave behind, to give my daughters.

No good offering the view
between here and Three Rock Mountain,
the blueness in the hours before rain, the long haze afterwards.
The ground I stood on was never really mine. It might not ever
                                                be theirs.

And gifts that were passed through generations –
silver and the fluid light left after silk – were never given here.

This is an island of waters, inland distances,
with a history of want and women who struggled
to make the nothing which was all they had
into something they could leave behind.

I learned so little from them: the lace bobbin with its braided mesh,
its oat-straw pillow and the wheat-coloured shawl
knitted in one season
to imitate another

are all crafts I never had
and can never hand on. But then again there was a night
I stayed awake, alert and afraid, with my first child
who turned and turned; sick, fretful.

When dawn came I held my hand over the absence of fever,
over skin which had stopped burning, as if I knew the secrets
of health and air, as if I understood them

and listened to the silence
and thought, I must have learned that somewhere.

John Burnside

By Pittenweem

> *One knows*
> *There is no end to the other world,*
> *no matter where it is.*
> Charles Wright

I HOME

We studied to love the cold,
to make a friend of it, to call it home,

since nothing else
was altogether true,

steeple, or pithead,
bellflower, grandmother's ring;

yet still we were expert
in thaw,

mapping the wetlands,
waiting for crowsfoot to blossom,

fighting the pull of rivers
on April nights,

till all the dreams we had
were dreams of water.

Now, on the fields
and the thrawn trees lining the ditch,

the new sun gathers and runs
like clarified butter,

and, perched on a fence post,
a buzzard extends its wings,

then settles back;
                    I'm not a threat to him:
a man without a gun, without a dog,

walking his boundary, measuring,
making good,

I'm not really bound to this place, but
here by choice:

pledged to the first thaw; visible;
out in the open;

accustomed to secrets
and keeping the best of myself

for private use:
a cold blade clenched in my fist

or a length of twine,
my body mapped and measured by the heft

of work that must be done
no matter what.

Springtime again:
                    the news all news of flood
and death by drowning,

a levee crumbling away,
a boat going under,

women and children
with faultlines of dread in their faces,

bloated bodies
sprawled on limbs of sand;

and yet, from a distance,
it's hard not to notice the beauty,

the stillness that falls,
the everyday chaos of flotsam,

and, out on a bridge of sandbags,
wed to the rain,

the rescue teams, still working in the dark,
each with his secret, and keeping the best of himself

for hope
          the way the coldest things
give hope:

floodwater, blizzard,
the numb girl pulled from the wreck

still breathing,
in the only home we have:

bone-cold, starlit,
plotted with kill-sites and whispers,

buzzards and starlings
drawn in, then turning away,

spawn in a dew-pond,
stitching the grass with desire.

There was something I heard in the wind,
geese, or the call of a vixen,
or something else, beyond vocabulary;

and sometimes, at night, I feel myself
alone in the dark and looking to see what there is
between the near field and the kitchen door:

the old familiars shifting in the grass
beyond the garden; mute ghosts come from the sea;
the gods that only stones and bulbs recall

rising like smoke and waiting to be found
in the cry of a bird, or the promise of midnight frost;
though nothing will come in a form I could recognise,

no story book figure, no cold face pressed to the glass,
no girl in the attic, weeping, or clutching a doll,
no eerie singing, out along the hedge

some August afternoon.
Tonight, when I stop to imagine, nothing is there,
or only a mist of rain on the left-over pea-sticks,

a glint of light, or something like a cry
that might be nothing;
                              only the other world
unending, yet lost throughout time

in a circle of light,
a murmur that comes through the wind,
a hand's-breadth, a wingspan,

arriving from nowhere, or conjured up out of the dark
between the near field and the kitchen door,
to sound me out, to comfort me with nothing.

III DIRT ROAD

Something that runs to copper
or cornflower blue,

a live creature bounding away
from the glare of my headlamps

and, when the engine stops, a sudden
quiet that waits to be filled

by owls, or cicadas;
though somebody else would say

it's only in the afterlife we get
to talk about such things:

the scent of diesel
misting on our fingers,

a motion in the sky
that never stops,

and how the brimming undergrowth is laced
with boundaries, the softness underfoot

a terminus
            that shifts
and wanders,

            though the end is all it seems:
another colour, not quite red, or mauve,

a trace of cold
more urgent than a kiss,

arriving, like some homespun messenger,
to isolate this waking from the dark.

IV HISTORY

Pilots and whalers, authorised privateers,
fugitives, botanists, ships' surgeons, makers of maps,
sailing from here, or further along the coast,
to parts unknown;
                                    or, half a mile inland,
the old-time celebrants
of seed and weather: tradesmen in their gloves
and aprons; blacksmiths, burnished by the heat
of dark, unending fires; the wandering
haberdasher, cycling round the farms
with cotton twills and satins for a dance;

for all of them, the predicate was home,
if not the world of others, then the world
of all they left unsaid; *that* inwardness:
the house behind the houses in their dreams,
the house of cold, the rooms of fern and bone,
the refuge in a squall, the proof in storms.

All afternoon I waited for the snow,
the horses in the near field staring off
to somewhere memorised: some open plain,
ice in the grass, the grass mapped out in song.
The old potato track, the Lochty line,
is frost and brambles now,
the rattle of old trains sealed in the wood
of fence posts, or that singing in the wires
that mark each neighbour's plot

of whins and stones.

I picture them, shipped in from tenements
and mining towns: mothers and eldest sons,
the casually employed, in hats and scarves,
wet hands numb with the cold
as they follow the tractors,
the life without end of lives that history
finds interchangeable:

                              my mother, say,
in her damp coat and hand-knitted sweater,
leading the way; me, stumbling over the clods
and wishing I was home beside the stove,
clothes hanging up to dry in our steaming kitchen,
the radio playing, those voices from somewhere else
announcing the songs we would hum,
as we counted the hours,
crossing the field, unseeing
and bright with the cold,
everything bleeding away,
to pulp and rain.

All afternoon, I waited for the ghosts
I wanted to find, shapes
shifting in the white
of blizzard,
              ghosts
not altogether dead, just *cold and gone*;
but when it came, the snow fell urgently
and for the sake of urgency alone,
empty and clear and quick, erasing the road,
erasing the deer-runs and verges, remaking the land
as something unknown and familiar, some holy ground:
the house behind the houses in my dreams,
standing apart, a little cube of lights
and singsong: music; voices from afar;

wind in the phone lines;
the hum of an idling machine.

V BEGINNING

The worst is to reach the end
and never know:
my mother,

dying, say,
pretending the future

existed, when all she had
was an infinite present,

a foreknowledge circling her eyes,
like cold, or soot,

                    a burial
rehearsed between her fingers;

or this old buzzard on the disused
railway line, unravelling his kill,

the winter that might be his last
unfolding around him:

sheep-tracks
and muddled snow,

and the deep sky over his head
unfastened

by the first true white
of stars.

No doubt the earth
forgets us, as we pass

from here to there:
the living and the dead

consanguine, vagrant,
blurring along the walls

like snowdrifts, or some
flicker in the wind,

but this
is neither end

nor resurrection,
only the subtler work

of being:
              birth
in *mutabilitie*,

the black
between the pinion and the snow,

the scattered flesh,
the sweet slur in the dew,

arriving
at a natural conclusion:

logos and water, navelwort,
singing bones,

scavenger warmth
emerging from the cold.

Luke Kennard

THE JOURNALIST'S PRAYER

Oh, that I could harness thought plantations;
Perfect villages of memory,
The tree, ponderous with ravens;
The plastic bread in a plastic oven –
A gentleman proclaiming it delicious,
Winking, offstage, that he might be debunked;
And I, with my thunderous notebook,
Emerging from the vault, yesterday.
I know where to kick a shark, I know
The graceful bull, the loathsome dove;
That their apparent tranquillity
Is rather silent, impotent terror.
May criticising me become forever redundant
That I might wake with a shriek of happiness.
May I never have to bury another leopard.
Let me be thought intelligent, even the kindest;
And when I am without sin,
Let me cast the first stone;
And when I am without pride,
Let them build a statue in my honour.

The Murderer

I take the murderer for coffee.
'Make sure you don't murder your coffee!'
I joke. He likes my jokes.

Later I swing a plank into his face:
This is to stop him enjoying himself –
Which is integral to the rehabilitation process.

His mouth trickles blood like a tap quarter-turned.
He likes my analogies. 'Hey, Murderer!'
I yell, '*Murdered* anyone recently?'

The murderer likes to play badminton.
When he loses, I say, 'That's what you get for being a murderer.'
When he wins, I say,

'I guess you got yourself in pretty good shape
Murdering all those people.'
I'm not about to let the murderer forget he's a murderer.

When I dance with the murderer I let him lead
Because he is the more proficient dancer –
'Just be careful not to murder me!' I tease.

The prison sits on the horizon like a great ash-tray –
When we travel I give him the window seat.
'Hey, murderer, would you like a sandwich?' I say,

'Or would you rather murder someone?'
The murderer eats his cheese and ham sandwich.
'The forecast is for snow,' I tell him.

The murderer has just had a haircut.
'Your new haircut makes you look like Judas,' I say.
That night we go to see a musical adaptation

Of the September 11th terrorist attacks.
It doesn't go down well – in fact the show
Is abandoned due to audience derision.

'Oh, I'm *sorry*,' cries the director.
'Is five years too soon for you people?'
The next day it is sunny, so we have a picnic

With French bread and olives and cheeses
And a box of wine. The breeze is cold.
'I think I will write a novel called:

My Picnic with a Murderer,' I say.
We stay out until the light is low and the grass is damp.
The murderer gets bitten by a red ant.

When we get home I dump the picnic basket
In the kitchen with the washing up and the half-eaten
Cans of beans. A half dead fly crawls up the window.

The murderer never cleans the house
Due to self-esteem issues.
He doesn't believe that he deserves a clean house:

He believes that the house should mirror his soul.
I take the murderer shopping for a new wardrobe.
'Let's get you spruced up,' I tell him.

I buy him a little sailor suit with *murderer* embroidered
On the collar. My mother's been calling again;
Somebody sold her a carpet she doesn't want.

The murderer has written a libretto.
'It's not bad, for a murderer,' I tell him.
'Maybe you could round up some other murderers

And they can perform it for you.'
We do not mention the libretto again, even when
The murderer refuses to be interviewed

For *True Crime* magazine. 'I'd have thought
That was right up your street,' I say.
'You know – crime, and all that.'

I have a separate telephone for talking to the murderer.
I call it The Disgusting Telephone.
The murderer likes to keep abreast of current affairs.

'You'll be pleased to hear there's been a natural disaster,'
I tell him. 'Over seven hundred dead.
I expect that's made your day, hasn't it?'

Every Tuesday we visit the Job Centre.
'Unfortunately nobody currently requires a murderer,'
I report. 'Still. There's always next week.'

The murderer smiles, patiently. On his birthday
I take the murderer to the best restaurant in town.
'Don't you know any other murderers we can invite?'

I ask. He doesn't reply, so I don't push the point.
'Here's to you, murderer!' I raise my champagne glass.
I'm thinking of taking up Yoga or something.

I pick up the murderer's girlfriend at the station.
'Have you travelled far?' I ask her.
'No,' she says. 'It should have been half an hour,

But a horse died on the tracks.
It took them three hours to remove it, poor creature.'
'A horse is rather like an unforgivable sin, isn't it?' I say.

She is wearing a dress made of shag-pile carpet;
She is drinking a can of orangeade.
She has another can of orangeade in her pocket.

'I can see you like orangeade,' I say,
'But what attracted you to the murderer?
Do you have some kind of a *thing* about murderers?'

She watches the raindrops on the passenger window.
'I hope *you're* not a murderer, too,' I say.
'One murderer in my life is quite enough for me.'

'Actually,' she says, quietly, 'I think we're *all* murderers.'
I brake for a red light. 'That's lucky,' I say.
'I imagine it would be difficult going out with a murderer

If you weren't a moral relativist.'
The murderer is watching a chat show and eating
His third tube of Oriental Spice flavour crisps.

His girlfriend gives him a can of orangeade.
He acknowledges her with a grunt.
'If you need me, I'll be checking my e-mails,' I say.

I am to be allocated a new murderer.
The conference takes place on a summer evening,
The undersides of seagulls illuminated by floodlights.

'God bless you, tiny flying cathedrals,' I mutter.
'You probably don't understand that. being a murderer,
But it's called a metaphor. It's a thing I use for talking
    about seagulls.'

I check-in the murderer with my coat.
The strip-lit foyer smells of sausage rolls,
Lined with posters for Renaissance art exhibitions

And unmanned tables selling audio-cassette interviews.
The notice boards hold more defunct announcements.
A bell rings and we climb the ladders to the auditorium.

I do not like my colleagues or their sweaters
Which appear to be decorated with an arcane form of
    sheet music.
Each time I look at their bellies or chests

I hear the antiphonal strains of ancient chants.
I do not like the speaker or the host;
Their boot-black hair and woollen bonhomie.

They say things like 'Watch this space!'
And 'Hold that thought!' when they are leaving
Temporarily to get a sandwich.

The murderers were left in a holding pen for reallocation,
Only someone forgot to lock the gate, so now they roam
The centre saying, 'How do you do?'

And 'I really enjoyed your talk.' I find my murderer sitting
Alone in the car park and I say, 'Come on murderer,
Let's go home.' Silently, he climbs into the passenger seat.

Jack Mapanje

THE SEASHELLS OF BRIDLINGTON NORTH BEACH
(for Mercy Angela)

She hated anything caged, fish particularly,
Fish caged in glass boxes, ponds, whatever;

'Reminds me of prisons and slavery,' she said;
So, when first she caught the vast green view

Of Bridlington North Beach shimmering that
English summer day, she greeted the sight like

A Sahara girl on parched feet, cupping, cupping,
Cupping the water madly, laundering her palms,

Giggling and laughing. Then rubbing the hands
On her skirt, she threw her bottom on the sandy

Beach and let the sea breathe in and out on her
As she relaxed her crossed legs – 'Free at last!'

She announced to the beach crowds oblivious;
And as the seascape rallied and vanished at her

Feet, she mapped her world, 'The Netherlands
We visited must be here; Norway, Sweden there;

Beyond that Russia!' Then gathering more sea-
shells and selecting them one by one, she turned

To him, 'Do you remember eating porridge from
Beach shells once?' He nodded, smiling at another

Memory of the African lakes they were forced to
Abandon. 'Someday, perhaps I'll take that home

To celebrate!' She said staring into the deep sea.
Today, her egg-like pebbles, her pearls of seashells

Still sparkle at the windowsill; her wishes still ring,
'Change regularly the water in the receptacles to

Keep the pebbles and seashells shining – you'll
See, it's a lot healthier than feeding caged fish!'

THE WEDDING OF JACARANDAS
(for Judith & Nicholas, January 2005)

'When the crocodiles of home
forced us unto the foreign lands
we are forever adopting, they hoped
we'd never discover how they blew
their noses above the rough waters
and believed we'd never again check
our fish traps for glistening tilapia
or sing and dance to our big dance –
but they were, as always, wrong!
For, today, as your shades of Zomba
jacarandas blossom, dear Judith,
happily wedded to shades of Masaka
jacarandas, dear Nicholas; as Christ
the King Catholic Church brushes
aside the dry brown dust of Kampala
city, my dear children, today you
shame mum and me for bothering
about the beasts of home when we
should have been dancing all along.

'Do not falter then, dear daughter,
we, your own blood, could not
have married you off to a pack of
stubborn wolves; and do not fear,
dear son, we could not have brought
you into another uncaring village
kraal! Remember, what love, what
pledges and promises brought us
here, remember the coffee beans
the elders from both sides cracked
in Kampala and Masaka, remember
how we broke the delicious chicken
baked in banana leaf satchels, how
the treasured friends who flew with

us saw the source of River Nile and
crossed the Equator myth – catching
the water twirling left, twirling right,
standing still – all for your wedlock.

'Do not forget, therefore, to bring
that golden shield of smile, love,
prayer and caring, upon which your
jacarandas were raised; let the delicate
shades of lilac you grew up on be
your armour to confront the tough
beetles you encounter in the lands
you are forever adopting; may that
ancestral cloud which suddenly broke
into rare showers on that dry and
hazy Masaka sky when we arrived
and curiously haloed your heads
as we parted, forever hug your lilac
dreams, with our eternal blessing!'

SCOTTISH POETRY LIBRARY
By leaves we live
5 Crichton's Close
Edinburgh
EH8 8DT
Tel 0131 557 2876

Sean O'Brien

Drains

In drains begin responsibilities.
        Joseph Chamberlain

Sites of municipal vaticination,
Vents for the stench of the underworld.
In dreams we are digested there
And 'in that Catholic belly curled'.

There we are sunk for Barbaricchio's crew
To heft upon their tuning-forks.
We dream too much. We talk too much.
The future of the market lies in corks.

Re-edify me, drains. Give me again
The under-city's grand designs.
Let me explore your slimy malls,
Your long drops and your flooded mines.

Some say the drains are heaven's guts,
Out progress intestinal.
Wherever peristalsis leads
The outcome will be final.

THE BRAZIER

Someone was up before dawn
To light the brazier by the path
Between the wood and the allotments.
It adds its slow grey smoke to fog,
As a choked pipe adds
Its trickle to a stagnant pool.
  I study the half-closed eyes of the brazier
In downtime. This too will pass,
I have it on authority.
  But who comes here to warm themselves?
The dead old men who dug this iron ground
Before we'd even heard of it?
  The brazier issues the idea of heat,
Like a twist of clear water
Fed into the murk of the pool.
I try to warm my hands,
But there is too much winter in the field.
  The brazier grows a cowl of smoke,
Then doffs it slowly, a magnifico
Assigned to this unfinished hell,
This foggy swamp of burning ice.
What was the sin? Austerity?
  This is the world we were promised, it seems,
Grey pastoral, an enclave in the North's
Built-over fields, a grave in all but name,
Among frostbitten beans and cabbage-stalks,
A world with one season, whose nights
Are moonless, starless intervals
Of cold within the cold, whose days
Begin and fade beneath the brazier's
Slow, grey-lidded, parsimonious gaze.

Adam Thorpe

ON HER BLINDNESS

My mother could not bear being blind,
to be honest. One shouldn't say it.

One should hide the fact that catastrophic
handicaps are hell; one tends to hear,

publicly, from those who bear it
like a Roman, or somehow find joy

in the fight. She turned to me, once,
in a Paris restaurant, still not finding

the food on the plate with her fork,
or not so that it stayed on (try it

in a pitch-black room) and whispered,
'It's living hell, to be honest, Adam.

If I gave up hope of a cure, I'd bump
myself off.' I don't recall what I replied,

but it must have been the usual sop,
inadequate: the locked-in son.

She kept her dignity, though, even when
bumping into walls like a dodgem; her sense

of direction did not improve, when cast
inward. 'No built-in compass,' as my father

joked. Instead, she pretended to ignore
the void, or laughed it off.

Or saw things she couldn't see
and smiled, as when the kids would offer

the latest drawing, or show her their new toy –
so we'd forget, at times, that the long,

slow slide had finished in a vision
as blank as stone. For instance, she'd continued

to drive the old Lanchester
long after it was safe

down the Berkshire lanes. She'd visit exhibitions,
admire films, sink into television

while looking the wrong way.
Her last week alive (a fortnight back)

was golden weather, of course,
the autumn trees around the hospital

ablaze with colour, the ground royal
with leaf-fall. I told her this, forgetting,

as she sat too weak to move, staring
at nothing. 'Oh yes, I know,' she said,

'it's lovely out there.' Dying has made her
no more sightless, but now she can't

pretend. Her eyelids were closed
in the coffin; it was up to us to believe

she was watching, somewhere, in the end.

INVALID

On the train out of Nuremberg
I shared a first-class carriage

with an old man who asked me to swap
seats, as he couldn't face

the direction in which the train was going
without turning faint thanks to a wound

in his head (really, a hole in which
he invited me to stick my thumb)

from a dose of shell at Stalingrad.
His fingers were burned to a claw

by frostbite; he was all raw victim –
nineteen when it happened – though German

and in the Werhmacht, then. His reward
was free travel, first class, *überall*

in Deutschland. Yes, his hole was deep
and on his skull, invisible under the hair.

A secret thing. A place where war had come
and gone, like a nightmare, like a devil's

print in stone: a tiny hoof
that left him unable to face that one direction

life rushed at him from, before plunging on.
I knew what he meant. It's easier

to sit with your back to things,
watch them glide away and dwindle

there where you've already been
into the long liquid of remembering.

Shortlisted Poems
The Felix Dennis Prize for Best First Collection

Joanna Boulter

Don't take those mittens off until you're called
to play your bit. Blow on your fingers, tuck
them in your armpits, beat this vicious cold
how best you can. Music's what matters. Look,

the carvings on the wall are rimmed with rime.
The keyboard's icy too. It hurts to play.
So what? Think of the music as a flame
to warm your spirit at. That's what I do.

There's counterpoint and cabbage soup, there's Bach
and badinage; and if that's not enough
you needn't stay. Okay, the winter's harsh.
And so am I. Get on and do your stuff.

The profs may make allowances. I don't.
And you delude yourself, for music can't.

PRELUDE

Endemic, this malaria of suspicion.
As if the land's one vast mephitic swamp,
rumours buzzing like mosquitoes. Someone
scratches an itch, and before you can say *Lubianka*
another poor devil's in quarantine.
It's a contagion. You can't tell who's clean.
Often they show no symptoms till they fall,
are lugged off, screaming, fainting, in the plague cart.
And the relatives, too – for every mother
queueing those lifetimes at the iron doors
a dozen cousins withdraw themselves from taint,
lay information for a talisman.
The witchfinders search for infection, stalk the streets,
all bone masks and blank eyes in the night.
And the lost behind those high walls dwindle away,
all bone masks, blank eyes, forgotten names.

Melanie Challenger

From THE SERVICE OF THE HEART

'Sleeping Beauty with Floating Roses', *1910*,
from a collection of memorial photographs.

What delights me is the part of me to become this girl –
Her outline an iceberg in the death-world,
Persevering fragilely like memories of passion.
Who wonders what she might have let slip to devour
Of the world's prospects? Bare possibility weighed down
By the logic of rotten fruit upon the garden floor.

Now, the ultraviolet womb is sunk beneath her,
Closing ranks upon the grail of another,
And her body cherishes not the disco-purple of those lips
Like a gentle handbag's clasp – instead elapse
The same generous tulips of flesh, as if her body of chance
Had always envied what she thought of as ugly, the corpse
Delighting in the swallowing of her inheritance:

The Sodom of her bruised heart, atrophied fruit of Eden.
O that I might love my unbeautying.

From THE SPARK OF TRANSGRESSION

I'm going to leave a heart in the earth
So it may grow and flower.

Leave your heart in the earth
Its gracious mandrake nature
Gives heirs to the rhapsodies of our reign.
Slender shoots stir the senseless mire,
    disturbing embedded caresses,
From whose overcast materials comes the rebirth

Of all that we have adored, all that we have dared
To pour scorn on, all that we have brushed aside,
The atomic rendering of a generation's obsessions –
The clay of the goylem. Liebniz's monads.
The beautiful imprimis, our lifeblood
In the bud. The earliest spark of our transgressions.

Leave your heart in the earth that it might bloom
To the body's thwarted openness,
Gospels unspoken in life expressing their feverishness
In the fraught whispering of leaves at the close
Of their affiliations. Attend to the hymn
Of life's cowardice cadenced in all that grows.

Leave your heart in the night soil that the land
Of its birth, forgiving its presence, might bless the roots'
Passage through the seams of man and beast
To the seat of the globe's mercy.   And beyond.
To a new aurora by whose kindlier radiance the fruits
Of our arrested affections swell to their feast.

Daljit Nagra

DARLING & ME!

Di barman's bell done dinging
        so I phone di dimply-mississ,
Putting some gas on cookah,
        bonus pay I bringin!

Downing drink, I giddily
        home for Pakeezah record
to which we go-go, tango,
        for roti – to kitchen – she rumba!

I tell her of poor Jimmy John,
        in apron his girlfriend
she bring to pub his plate of
        chicken pie and dry white

potato! Like Hilda Ogden,
        Heeya, eaht yor chuffy dinnaaah!
She huffing off di stage
        as he tinkle his glass of Guinness.

We say we could never eat
        in publicity like dat, if we did
wife advertisement may need
        of solo punch in di smack.

I pull her to me – my skating
        hands on her back are Bolero
by Torvill and Dean. Giggling
        with bhangra arms in air

she falling for lino, till I
       swing her up in forearm!
Darling is so pirouettey with us
       for whirlwind married month,

that every night, though by day
       we work factory-hard, she always
have disco of drumstick in pot.
       Hot. Waiting for me.

A Prelude to Suka's Adventures from the Board Room

He was the first from our farms on a cheap boat ride to Britain.
        Within a year of work, showered
with overtime, he sent home his pounds for an Enfield bike.
        Dripping in black and silver
it posed in the courtyard. Our scooters farting on the parched
        soil as we left-behinds would meet
to be drawn by the pull from the flood of his letters that swore
        on swift returns for a small price.

I crossed the sea, like those Englishmen who made their names
            abroad,
        for his damp and graffiti'd house
where he threw up a panel of chip wood on the bath, and titled
        this my bedroom. Whispering
there's a stream of shift-working men, sleeping days or nights,
        swamping the shared space.
Then he sucked the chain on his steaming piss. In the kitchen
        he fed me cardboard chapattis.

I had left my wife, and the drip of mail from wherever
        at my village postal job,
for this once always-drunk, street-sweeper's boy made good.
        When I asked about the button-
pushing work he'd gushingly written of, I almost choked
        at his head on a body of stick,
at the ash of ghostly hair and the sunken eyes
        as he laughed and laughed through his yellow teeth.

Eleanor Rees

Night Vision

An open moon; burr of grass.
Last reaches of the spilt day
ending, the last
quiet pitch heard
in deep woods. Wet sod of dirt.
Scent of the sun's fire
passing field ruts and furrows,
seedlings, coiled roots, hedgerows;
flight of night-bird
turning tail into a sea breeze
beak battened to the north.

*

Cloud – now stone in ocean in undertow –
drops from night above the city
into an unseen sea,
at edges of membrane and sinew.
Wade through sky. Perforate.
Pebbles of rain on pitted tarmac
clutter the way home;
night-splashed, corroded.

*

A cold touch in a bleeding house.
An open door. Sores.

And I dream you are the rising sun:

where are your bones, baby? Where are your bones?
        I've hurt for you – for your nights.
        Each turn and flat-packed mile

walked to catch the drift and knack of ends
        and fugitive ends.
Back alleys of the city burn.
Night boils outside the window.
The streets smoulder as morning comes.

ANDRASTE'S HAIR

In the woods they are burning her hair
                          three of them
they light it with a match
and she lets them
she lets them burn her hair.

Watches the ends smoulder.
Watches the ends curl her curls
curl up like leaves.

She lets them burn her hair.
There are long dark shadows
                    between trees
                        like corridors
blocked with boulders.

– The area is cordoned off. –

She let them burn her hair.

 – The area is cordoned off. –

When the sun splits open

the gaps between trees

and the sun slices into the scene

they see:

that she let them burn her hair.

    *

The light opens up the morning.

A plait lain out on the end of the bed
                              like a rope
several metres long it hung there
swaying
                    tied with a yellow bow.

It belongs to no one now
lopped off at the nape of the neck.

The door is closed.

　　*

Arms raised to hug the sun
woman
                    eyes like sods
ratchet-nosed, craggy
hatchet arms creak and clank

lady

sleeping under sunless light

another sun gone

reaching obedient: she dreams.

　　*

From among the ashes
from what had not burnt
            gathered to a mass
of brown turf gathered
            her hair
and carried

– a cloud in her arms –
and carried
      to the river
      her hair
to spread in the warp of water.

The light smooth and silting.
The forest behind –
      remember
too much   too much
      dark cannot exist?
      The sun swings to the right.
She went left
      to the river
      old dirt track
stepping over grass
hair taken down to depth.

In the forest they look for her.

Now,

she walks along the path by the river
her hair in her hands
      to deliver
what had been taken
      to the river
      to the water
the smooth strand that curves its path
over the head of the hill.

Something subsides.
Something has passed.
Behind in the forest
          in half dark heaving afternoon
they claw at earth

scratch around for a trace
                            and further
in the woods
search through evidence
make lists of explanations
make lists of reasons
for her absence.

The sun guides steps,
        footfalls
            imprint on soil.

    *

It wasn't about who was listening.
If anyone was listening
        – to the song not the words –
speaking would mean silence
        – dead ears dead ears –
but variation
the pull and placing
in a line brimmed to full
            with evocation
was almost love and almost listening.

Quiet response to quiet sound.

    *

A song heard in the forest days later

burbled

made a young boy cry.

Wrapped round trees
stayed, not moving,
                              just hung
a stopping place.

We could meet
in the woods by the river
stand eye to eye
in the stopping place
                    and wait
words curdling our bones
                    to stone
          be petrified
                              in sound
a single drum beat, one long groan.

While she walks
a path behind her concertinas
each stride a fragile weight
that
          pushes up the earth,
turf over grass over turf.

Know how
it is now to be stone now
to know how to finish.

Listen, she'll break you.

Will you follow?

Shortlisted Poems
The Forward Prize for Best Single Poem
in memory of Michael Donaghy

David Harsent

THE HUT IN QUESTION

Rain, midnight rain, nothing but the wild rain
On this bleak hut, and solitude, and me...
    Edward Thomas, 'Rain'

And here it is, slap on the co-ordinates,
nothing special of course,
a tar-paper roof (is it?) nailed to sloping slats,
a door that goes flush to the floor, and grates
when you draw it back. Weather-worn, half-hidden by gorse
in full fire, it being that time of year; the window
thick with cobwebs, clarty candyfloss;
a smell of rot; things spongy underfoot.

Being here alone is easiest.
There are songbirds in the sedge
(I think it is) and a wind to clout the reeds, a test
of the place, as are these clouds: a long dark flow
pulling fast and heavy off the ridge...
Easiest given what we make of quest,
its self-regard, its fearsome lost-and-found, its need to know
the worst and wear its sorrows like a badge.

Do you get what I mean if I speak of light – half-light –
that seems to swarm: a mass
of particles folding and rolling as if you stood too close
to a screen when the image dies? The edge
of night... those forms that catch and hold
just at the brink where it's nearly but not quite.

I see, now, by that light. Rain finally coming in, the day
falling short, adrift in shades of grey,
and nowhere to get to from here, or so I guess,
with distances fading fast,

with the road I travelled by a thinning smudge,
with all that lay between us bagged and sold,
with voices in under the door that are nothing more nor less
than voices of those I loved, or said I did,
with nothing at all to mark
fear or fault, nothing to govern loss,
and limitless memory starting up in the dark.

Lorraine Mariner

Thursday

I'm trying to get to work earlier and make
the short walk from Fenchurch Street Station
to the tube at Tower Hill where a guard
is pulling across the gate and commuters
are being evacuated through the gap
and he says it might be closed for ten minutes
half an hour and I think typical walk back
the way I came and on towards Monument
where it's closed again and this guard says
power failure so I walk towards Bank posting
a birthday card to my sister's boyfriend and at
the entrance to Bank it's the same so I phone
my mum who I know will have the radio on
but she says there's nothing on the travel news
you should get a bus to Victoria so I locate
a bus going to Victoria and follow it
to the bus stop and join the crowd that's formed
to wait for the next one and finally it comes
but it's jammed and I watch with admiration
as people with more balls than I'll ever have
leap on through the exit doors until the driver
gets wise and shuts them so I go and find
another bus stop and settle for a bus to Waterloo
with a seat and tell myself I'm not late yet
I'm getting a different view of the city and then
I hear the man behind say explosion and coming
down the stairs a text arrives from my friend
at work asking if I'm ok and so I phone her
and tell her I'm fine and ask her which is the best
bus to catch to Pimlico and then I try my mum
but now she's engaged and I'm standing opposite
the Shell building where my grandma worked
hoping for a 507 and my mum rings and says

it's bad but all my family members are safe
in their offices and I'm not to get on any more
buses so I start walking through the sirens
aiming for the building where my desk is waiting
exactly the way I left it yesterday evening.

Alice Oswald

a poem for a nearly dried-up river

Very small and damaged and quite dry,
a Roman Waternymph made of bone
tries to summon a river out of limestone.

Very eroded faded,
her left arm missing and both legs from the knee down,
a Roman Waternymph made of bone
tries to summon a river out of limestone.

Exhausted, utterly worn down,
a Roman Waternymph made of bone,
being the last known speaker of her language,
she tries to summon a river out of limestone.

Little distant sound of dry grass. Try again.

A Roman Waternymph made of bone,
very endangered now,
in a largely unintelligible monotone,
she tries to summon a river out of limestone.

Little distant sound as of dry grass. Try again.

Exquisite bone figurine with upturned urn,
in her passionate self-esteem, she smiles, looking sideways.
She seemingly has no voice but a throat-clearing rustle
as of dry grass. Try again.

She tries leaning,
pouring pure outwardness out of a grey urn.

Little slithering sounds as of a rabbit man in full night gear.
Who lies so low in the rickety willow-herb
that a fox trots out of the woods
and over his back and away. Try again.

She tries leaning,
pouring pure outwardness out of a grey urn.
Little lapping sounds. Yes.
As of dry grass secretly drinking. Try again.

Little lapping sounds yes
as of dry grass secretly drinking. Try again.

Roman bone figurine,
year after year in a sealed glass case,
having lost the hearing of her surroundings,
she struggles to summon a river out of limestone.

Little shuffling sound as of approaching slippers.

Year after year in a sealed glass case
a Roman Waternymph made of bone,
she struggles to summon a river out of limestone.

Pause. Little shuffling sound as of a nearly dried-up woman,
not really moving through the fields,
having had the gleam taken out of her
to the point where she resembles twilight. Try again.

Little shuffling clicking.
She opens the door of the church.
Little distant sounds of shutaway singing. Try again.

Little whispering fidgeting of a shutaway congregation
wondering who to pray to.
Little patter of eyes closing. Try again.

Very small and damaged and quite dry,
a Roman Waternymph made of bone,
she pleads she pleads a river out of limestone.

Little hobbling tripping of a nearly dried-up river
not really moving through the fields,
having had the gleam taken out of it
to the point where it resembles twilight.
Little grumbling shivering last-ditch attempt at a river
more nettles than water. Try again.

Very speechless, very broken old woman,
her left arm missing and both legs from the knee down,
she tries to summon a river out of limestone.

Little stoved-in sucked-thin
low-burning glint of stones
rough-sleeping and trembling and clinging to its rights.

Victim of Swindon.
Puddle midden.
Slum of overgreened foot-churn and pats
whose crayfish are cheap tool kits
made of the mud stirred up when a stone's lifted.

It's a pitiable likeness of clear running,
struggling to keep up with what's already gone:
the boat the wheel the sluice gate,
the two otters larricking along. Go on.

And they say oh they say
in the days of better rainfall
it would flood through five valleys,
there'd be cows and milking stools
washed over the garden walls
and when it froze, you could skate for five miles. Yes go on.

Little loose-end shorthand unrepresented
beautiful disused route to the sea,
fish path with nearly no fish in.

Carole Satyamurti

The Day I Knew I Wouldn't Live for Ever

The summer I conquer water, I taste power again
like learning to walk, but this time I'll remember –
being that proud impossible thing, a swimmer;
ecstatic, buoyed up, striking out and out,
swooping with the waves, diving through.

I flip to look back, and the beach is painting-
by-numbers – coloured patches so small I can't tell
which are my family. I was one of those bright dots
and now my space has closed behind me.
I could not exist, and there'd be no difference.

The sea starts to jostle and leer, I've swallowed
knowledge more serious than I knew there was.
This is too vast for me, and I'm swimming hard,
but the dots and patches don't get bigger. No point
shouting, I am invisible – too far out for anything

but keeping on, though without hope, with no
breath, and aching arms. But my life so far
doesn't pass before me like the teacher said, and now
my feet nudge seaweed, and I wade, jelly-legged
and look for our umbrella, and find it.

Nothing has happened. They haven't missed me.
It's cold. My knitted swimsuit is bleeding magenta
into powder blue. My parents set up cricket stumps.
They don't know it's all the same, who wins.
The sun makes them cheerful. I am so much older.

Myra Schneider

GOULASH

A crucial ingredient is the right frame of mind
so abandon all ideas of getting on. Stop pedalling,
dismount, go indoors and give yourself masses of time.
Then begin by heating a pool of oil in a frying pan
and, Mrs. Beeton style, take a dozen onions
even though the space you're working in is smaller
than the scullery in a Victorian mansion. Pull off
the papery wrappings and feel the shiny globes' solidity
before you chop. Fry the segments in three batches.
Don't fuss about weeping eyes, with a wooden spoon
ease the pieces as they turn translucent and gold.
When you've browned but not burnt the cubes of beef
marry meat and onions in a deep pan, bless the mixture
with stock, spoonfuls of paprika, tomato purée
and crushed garlic. Enjoy the Pompeian-red warmth.
Outside, the sun is reddening the pale afternoon
and you'll watch as it sinks behind blurring roofs,
the raised arms of trees, the intrepid viaduct.
In the kitchen's triumph of colour and light the meat
is softening and everything in the pot is seeping
into everything else. By now you're thinking of love:
the merging which bodies long for, the merging
that's more than body. While you're stirring the stew
it dawns on you how much you need darkness.
It lives in the underskirts of thickets where sealed buds
coddle green, where butterflies folded in hibernation,
could be crumpled leaves. It lives in the sky that carries
a deep sense of blue and a thin boat of moon angled
as if it's rocking. It lives in the silent larder and upstairs
in the airing cupboard where a padded heart pumps
heat, in the well of bed where humans lace together.
Time to savour all this as the simmering continues,
as you lay the table and place at its centre a small jug

in which you've put three tentative roses and sprigs
of rosemary. At last you will sit down with friends
and ladle the dark red goulash onto plates bearing
beds of snow-white rice. As you eat the talk will be bright
as the garnets round your neck, as those buried
with an Anglo-Saxon king in a ship at Sutton Hoo,
and the ring of words will carry far into the night.

Jean Sprackland

From THE BIRKDALE NIGHTINGALE

Bufo calamito – the Natterjack toad

On Spring nights you can hear them
two miles away, calling their mates
to the breeding place, a wet slack in the dunes.
Lovers hiding nearby are surprised
by desperate music. One man searched all night
for a crashed spaceship.

For amphibians, they are terrible swimmers:
where it's tricky to get ashore, they drown.
By day they sleep in crevices under the boardwalk,
run like lizards from cover to cover
without the sense to leap when a gull snaps.
Yes, he can make himself fearsome,
inflating his lungs to double his size.
But cars on the coast road are not deterred.

She will lay a necklace of pearls in the reeds.
Next morning, a dog will run into the water and scatter them.
Or she'll spawn in a footprint filled with salt rain
that will dry to a crust in two days.

Still, when he calls her and climbs her
they are well designed. The nuptial pads on his thighs
velcro him to her back. She steadies beneath him.

The puddle brims with moonlight.
Everything leads to this.

Highly Commended Poems

2007

Louise Adjoa Parker

RAG DOLL

How they throw her to one another
these men she goes to,
and laugh as she soars between them
like a rag doll,
all long cotton arms and
woolly braids trying their best
to stream gracefully in the air.

As she lands at their feet
they prod life into her, these men.
When they call her a beauty she smiles,
her painted dolly-pink mouth not quite reaching
her black spider-lashed eyes.

She tries to suck
drops of love from them, this doll-girl,
like a baby sucks milk,
tries to fill the hole in her cotton-wool heart,
wants the smell of sea-salt sweat
to take the place of her tears.

How prettily she flits between them
this woman-doll, a butterfly basking
in a sun of admiration
though she wakes each lonely morning,
with all her stuffing gone.

Tiffany Atkinson

ZUPPA DI CECI

In chipped English she told me
that to get mine like hers   Well
    I'm just too flash-in-the-pan
These things take time   Chick-peas alone
    must be soaked overnight then simmered for hours
while you stand at the stove with a slow spoon
    skimming off scum   only then a hope in hell
you'll get the rest of the ingredients to sit
    on the right staves   Though
what this has to do with you
    slipping out in the crease of night like
a dropped stitch   I can't think   just
    the kitchen window's black slab
where I stand sucking cream from the lip
    of an old spoon   a platter of reheated stars
and last night's moon served cold

John Barnie

Easter 3000

People said, Cover her face; we cannot have
her looking down at us like this; it was done;
still, it was a woman in the attitude of a

god; people said, We cannot have this at all;
this is the wrong scenario; women are always accessories
after the fact; why does she want to put us

through this ordeal; does she think she
can persuade us this is right; come here to
die in a woman's unsuitable form; this

is outrageous, a back-to-front world;
the sun won't stop for her, it will go
on in a masterful way through the sky till

she dies, and the moon will come up like
the sun's cold calf, stillborn and unwept for;
we have had enough of this; help us to

pull her down; this was never ordained, god
has no daughters, only a mild-faced son
for whom snowdrops bow their heads in winter;

I left and went home, and closed the door; the
news was on, with details of the final assault on the
city; I had to look away from the mothers, in old

clothes and headscarves; they are always the last to
understand; they bore the sons who must die,
who beheaded captured soldiers made to kneel in

sand, a blotter for their blood and humiliation;
the mothers cry for bread, for their sons,
the raped daughters who will drag shame through snow

to the graveyards; government-in-exile is already
planning the memorial, two billowing sails of blue-
glazed brick in the desert, like cupped ears,

for the troops to march past on Martyrs' Day
when this is over, and the city in our hands again;
I flicked channels, but none had news of the woman.

Suzanne Batty

SHRINK

Give me a shrinker of heads.
Shrink mine. Make it
a pinhole camera
with views of the country.

Make it a padded box
just big enough for a child's head.
Draw dark curtains across its face.
Cut small holes, for views of the stars.

Make it a foot-sized piece of earth
where purple marsh flowers creep.
Make it small and safe enough to sleep in.
Give it views of mountain tracks, green and vertical.

Make it compact. And airtight.
Let nothing out or in.
Make it as unassuming as plastic.
Let it be passed around. Let it be patted.

Give it a kind word.
Let it forget.
Give it the kiss of a black dog.
Give it another cigarette.

Let it be tragic. A song of despair.
But make it short. And to the point.

Nazand Begikhani

AN ORDINARY DAY

The security officer
got up early
put on his white shirt
had honey toast with nuts
kissed his three children
hugged his wife passionately
and left for work

At his desk
sat ten files
of ten men to be shot
He signed them
while drinking mint tea

At ten o'clock
he ordered the shooting
got angry over a gunman who missed his target
Taking out his pistol
he fired at the missed target ten times

Before the end of his shift
he visited the mothers of the ten shot men
ordered each to pay 100 dinars
for the cost of the bullets that killed their sons

In the evening
he celebrated his brother's birthday

At night
on the surface of a mirror
he saw a drop of blood trickling down to his feet
He tried to wash it
the trickle rose to his chest

Where does the difference lie between the killer and killed?

Anne Carson

WALKS FOR GIRLS AND BOYS
for RC

1 HURON RIVER

We walked by the river its arms all gold
in winter sun like tin.
Workshops of afternoon hummed along elsewhere.
We noted ice at the shore
and ice on plants
and ice from the light fixtures under the railway bridge exploding –
Squid, you said.
Time toppled past us.
There were no trains, no sunset.
Geese lapped at an edge, eyes inward on their sunk city.

2 THE POOL IN WINTER

Walking to the pool in winter I think of you.
And sway on them (thoughts) in the water too, blue, ablaze, you,
who once asked me
Do you ever swim really fast?
and I, wanting to be great to you,
said *Oh yes*, busily and pretended to laugh.
The pool has a deep clear sky like a marsh.
Bright as tongues is every light.
So I go on, my life goes, a few lies, a sweep of love, lap
after lap, ordinary motion and something else sent
past vast glass out of sight.

3 CHICAGO

Shrieks (white) and shades (suede) of dirty cold.
I walked down Montrose to the shore of the lake.
Past a shut Park Bait Shop and a boat
named *Temperance II,*
boat named *Mr Bright Eye,*
mud-knobbed fields,
rusted-out barbecue from medieval times.
Dog on the beach cavorting bleakly.
Lake is as ugly as a motel room.
Walls don't meet. Stains sag. One angel yawns in a horny heaven.
Against north wind I struggle back to where I was warm when I woke.
On the teapot a note from you about breathing.

4 WILD SEX

I walked to a coast.
The moon was in tumult.
It reminded me of walking down the alley where (you pointed) the
pile of bricks
used to be,
in the days when hookers came in from the street
and built a bit of a wall there
to take their tricks behind.
Each morning Dave (landlord) unbuilt the wall.
He never put the bricks anywhere else, like
inside.
It reminded me of a feeling of 'sudden school' I get
whenever men mention hookers
casually.
It reminded me of the word *glissando.*

James Caruth

This Man

The past is an empty café terrace.
                Eavan Boland

I am not this man

who sits in a railway café, watching
dark pools of rain on the terrace
catch the street lights' oily stain
as a Manchester evening spreads like a bruise.

It's not me who taps an unlit cigarette on a table,
or stares at the dregs in a coffee cup
while her face steals into my eyes
soft-footed like a burglar.

I don't try to map the city's familiar parts;
cheap hotels, the bars where we once met
like thieves, unpicking the seams of our hearts,
trading secrets of each other's lives
while the whispered vowels of her name
rained down on the rush-hour traffic.

And when a voice whines over the feedback on the PA
it's not me who has a train to catch.
I don't light another cigarette, or push my cup away
as outside on the terrace dark pools of rain
catch the street lights' oily stain and a Manchester evening
closes, tender as a bruise.

Ian Caws

Apple Day

Singular in a plural world,
my thoughts bed down. Then there are the apples
    in a weather turned mild,
apples on stalls, between shade on the grass
and sun crossing noiseless trees in ripples.
    We celebrate each thing that grows
        but mainly apples. Peeled,

    baked, picked and fallen, leaves on stems,
apples all in a day, that glowed with light,
    survived the summer storms.
There is happiness that comes of this,
there is a calm in the year turning late
    that I feel in the touch of these
        apples. And old customs

    of which brown, bearded men tell us,
we will mean to observe but will forget
    as nights chill and we gaze
down the long silences. We will return
to other apple days, will find the gate
    to old fields and whistle a tune
        that brings good memories,

    sets free all things necessary
for single minds in a plural world.
    We will look on starry
midnights and will remember the apples
in their baskets, their trays, and stretch to hold
    cider jugs as firelight dapples
        solidity away.

Jennifer Copley

Ten Places Where I See My Mother

Mondays, in the kitchen, her arms all suds.
I peer through steam but she's disappeared
till I see her in the yard, pegging sheets.
Later she'll be upstairs, taking off her wet blue dress
or coming out of the bathroom saying,
Don't use too much paper. We're quite low.

In the dark she's in different places:
the end of my bed, the space by the wardrobe,
picking up my clothes.
Fuzzy yellow light runs in ribbons
from her head to her heels.
Her footprints glow for ages after she's gone.

Today she's in the greenhouse
wearing gloves that are far too big
and the old straw hat.
I tap on the glass but she looks right through me.
I wish she'd smile, come close,
stroke back the fringe from my forehead.

Sundays, I see her under the earth,
peacefully asleep, her mouth slightly open,
but she comes to when I start arranging flowers.
Going home in the car, she sits beside me
folding the cellophane to use again,
winding the string round her little finger.

Nick Drake

c/o THE SEA AT PATEA
(in memory of Paul Winstanley)

I'd guess you thought of your life as a book
Of short stories, unpublished, their integrity
Ghosted by the rejection letters you kept
And replied to; or so I believe, who figured
In the months we coincided in the Alpujarras;
You in a derelict mill, in the one deckchair
Placed at the edge of a doorway into air
And evening light, the steps long gone, below
God's handful of scattered river rocks,
The river always awol but for the glints
Of currents in the silver of the stones;
In the distance, balanced terraces
Of oranges, olives, and white villages –
Almost, perhaps, an image of your ideal
Of a good life for all; food, land, dignity,
The kind of thing we'd drink to – I was young,
You were wiser – in the local wine
Rough as the tire-treads of our hippy sandals.
Then with your habitual economy
You packed yourself, your books, stones, recipes,
And hundreds of tapes into the old green tin
Of the favoured 2CV, and moved on again...
After a few letters we lost touch –
Until your memorial, and here you are
In photographs as everybody knew you;
Bald, bespectacled, moustached, that careful smile,
Like a comic we knew better than to name;
Lover of music, and bacon; detester of tissues;
And all the other stories I didn't know;
Pink Floyd roadie, potter, furniture maker,
Greenpeace engineer, political letter-writer;
'A life,' as you once wrote, 'seen as a whole –

As much as there was ever going to be.'
And finally here's the fisherman with his trophies
In the soft fawn cowboy hat now laid to rest
Beneath the cuttings of the local man
Who died, fishing, on New Year's Day. My dear,
(As you would say) I know it's far too late
To write a letter of any kind but this,
But I must, if only to stamp and post
With its best wishes and conditionals,
To Paul Winstanley c/o the Sea at Patea,
Your final and unchanging home address.

Sasha Dugdale

SONG OF A WANDERER

I am fearless. Fearlessness was seeded in me
In a small flat where all the talk was children's babble
And soft spider replies: *doggie, choochoo, baba*
And the kitchen clattered and shook with gravy
Boiling over. The bread rose
The meat bubbled in the heat, and crooked spiderfingers
Laid the pastry ring across the seething curd.
I was fearless with wanting to dress my own small body
Walk with long, straight legs down to the street
Before the vegetables, ready mashed and served,
Before the napkin, tucked into my skirt.

But wherever I go I find the same sweet harem
Cloysome to my heart. The same old women and the babies
The same babble. I taste the same smell of meat
From high-up windows. I watch the same old fingers
Kneading bread and see the ancient ring mark on the crust.
And when they ask me, 'Why not have a rest?' on some bed
So high and soft and melting, I say, 'Yes. I'm really very tired.'
And unroll, in a headache of a dream, my limbs
So weary from their walking. Yes, I am captive
To the pie crust and the stove, the women and their talking,
The children's little grip.

Ian Duhig

('Douce dame débonaire')

Follow your bright love, unlucky shadow
    whose comeliness is black
    from sun borne on your back –
yet follow your bright love, unlucky shadow.

The sun can quicken as she seems to stand
    a seedling Campion,
    that shadow's champion;
the old hand followed with this second hand.

Shadow with your hand, unhappy lover
    then close round your own dove;
    be dovecote, nest and glove:
what light has veiled, let darkness now uncover.

Discover what man most loves is himself:
    be warmed by your own sun
    in loving number one,
a love that will not leave you on the shelf.

Turn your gnomon to your source of light:
    the fall awaits the proud,
    for all of us, the shroud;
so come like God, alone, and in the night.

Helen Dunmore

To My Nine-Year-Old Self

You must forgive me. Don't look so surprised,
perplexed, and eager to be gone,
balancing on your hands or on the tightrope.
You would rather run than walk, rather climb than run
rather leap from a height than anything.

I have spoiled this body we once shared.
Look at the scars, and watch the way I move,
careful of a bad back or a bruised foot.
Do you remember how, three minutes after waking
we'd jump straight out of the ground floor window
into the summer morning?

That dream we had, no doubt it's as fresh in your mind
as the white paper to write it on.
We made a start, but something else came up –
a baby vole, or a bag of sherbet lemons –
and besides, that summer of ambition
created an ice-lolly factory, a wasp trap
and a den by the cesspit.

I'd like to say that we could be friends
but the truth is we have nothing in common
beyond a few shared years. I won't keep you then.
Time to pick rosehips for tuppence a pound,
time to hide down scared lanes
from men in cars after girl-children,

or to lunge out over the water
on a rope that swings from that tree
long buried in housing –
but no, I shan't cloud your morning. God knows
I have fears enough for us both –

I leave you in an ecstasy of concentration
slowly peeling a ripe scab from your knee
to taste it on your tongue.

Kate Edwards

Parallel Universes

He, pondered on the nature of infinity.
She, tried to paint infinity on a large canvas.
He dwelt in a singular world of quarks and mesons.
She lived in a physical world of paints and colour.
When he started speaking of 'charm' and 'beauty'
she thought they'd found at last a common interest
until he explained they were even smaller particles of matter.
When he was energised, she would be tired and paint-splashed,
he explained it in terms of Pauli's exclusion principle concerning
fermions, which can't be in the same energy state at once.
She threw cobalt blue and crimson madder onto flake white
which she had to admit looked nothing like infinity.
He went to a conference and spoke of anti-matter,
she overheard some talk about the curvature of space
so she pinned a sheet of paper to the wall and, with a brush,
drew a large curve beginning at the bottom corner.
She reached the edge of the paper before the top of the curve,
nowhere for the brush to go, so she carried on along the wall
and out of the open door where she found only air to paint on
where the brush left no mark and she had to give up.
He was furious about the Prussian Blue on the wall.
She told him it was only made of protons and neutrons.
He told her not to speak of what she did not understand.
The argument that followed was similar in nature
to the Big Bang in sound and fury, and afterwards
they expanded silently and swiftly away from each other.
He became excited about looking for the Grand Unified Theory
with the serious men he met at conferences, and String Theories
seemed the way to go. She brought him a ball of string
from the garden shed, and said he and she could be grand and
        unified.
He nearly strangled her with the string, then started studying
some long document about dimensions and subatomic particles.

She threw paint in handfuls at the canvas, Burnt Sienna,
Viridien, Chrome Yellow, Spanish Ochre, Indigo, Ivory Black.
One day she took her smallest brush with the finest point
and painted an infinitesimal dot in the centre of a blank wall.
At last she was satisfied that she had painted infinity.
When he returned he said what she had painted was nothing.
Very timidly she suggested that perhaps that is what infinity may be.

Elaine Feinstein

LONDON
for Natasha

A full ginger moon hangs in the garden.
On this side of the house there are no stars.
When I go to bed, I like to soothe myself with
streetlights, lit windows and passing cars.

When my grandchild comes to sleep over
I find we share the same preference.
She doesn't want to draw the curtains either.
I like to look out on my town, my London...

Have you seen London from above? she asks me.
It's like a field of lights. And her grey eyes widen.
Her eight-year-old spirit is tender as blossom.
Be gentle to her now, ferocious London.

Annie Freud

THE MANIPULATION OF WORDS

I jot one down and, like a sunbather,
it turns and looks at me as if to say,
OK, you've written me down. Fine!
Go and amuse yourself somewhere!

And here I am now on this beach,
strewn with the limbs of old loves,
the crumpled newspapers of new love,
his crossword, my striped windbreak.

I wander down the line of surf
pocketing debris that I've pocketed before,
the half-sunk shells and flattened ovoids,
the orange and blue twists of chandler's cord.

The lozenge of this brick, worn smooth,
disparages my urge to signify
and insists there's nothing to improve,
for it's a brick that's unlike any other,

as I was, when I loved another,
and everything he loved about me then...
even though I knew he didn't care.
With all my force, I lob it out to sea.

Cynthia Fuller

THEY SAID

They said that I must let him go,
that war is just, that I must trust
in God, and send him off rejoicing.

I think how thin his shoulders are,
the milky skin, the knobs of bone
as he bends to wash his face.

I think how he stands at the mirror,
my sharp rebukes, his clothes
just so, his wink at his vanity.

Don't baby him. His father's words,
He'll be a mother's boy. My gentle son,
I pray you are not fit enough to serve.

I wait for letters, read and re-read,
try to see what he isn't saying
in his tales of boots and parades.

I try to picture him lining up
for 'fumigation', 'inoculation',
and all I think of is disease.

He says the meals make him sick.
I know shop work didn't fit him
for marching with a full pack.

He has learnt to use a bayonet.
He makes it sound an adventure,
even the drilling and cleaning of kit.

He writes of 'musketry' and I see
all the guns that will point at him.
You must be proud, the neighbours say.

Don't worry over me dear Mother.
It's worse at night in the quiet house
when I cannot find my faith.

John Fuller

From THE SOLITARY LIFE

33 THE MEDITATION

Still as I am, it is the nearby stream
That carries me. The mind slides over stones
In little disconnected moods that seem
Like water as it imitates the tones
Of confidential speech: interminable
Narrative about some past event,
Inconsequential, self-important babble
That lulls an anaesthesia of assent.
The stream is speaking of its origin
A field or two above, that much is clear.
That always was its subject, is so still,
And will be till at last the sun goes in
And there is no one left alive to hear
It take its idle gossip down the hill.

34 THE FUTURE

As from the highest hills the heather's sprue
Pales to the purplish distance of the sea
And the effusive stream enlarges to
The silver windings of the estuary,
So we are certain that the future brings
A largeness with that vagueness and a kind
Of sublimation of the little things
That constitute the hunger of the mind.
Then, we assure ourselves, our purposes
Will be fulfilled and all dissatisfactions
Resolved into a settled state of being
When the last irritating error is
Discovered, every detail of our actions,
Like a long calculation, now agreeing.

Tess Gallagher

BLACK BEAUTY
for Ray

Pain added to pain it would have been,
to bring forward too soon
the beautiful unripe "us together" scenes.
So memory learned something from the dawn
about getting night out of the way,
letting dark be dark,
like the white heart of the apple
before it is broken open
to the miniature damp cathedral of its
even darker seeds.

There we are again
on the side-throne of the King Cole Bar
eating goblets of raspberries in February
at the St. Regis Hotel. This was between
renovations, after the skating rink, before
Lespinasse, and yes, it's true – the demolition
of that very room. Like memory, or at least
its corridor – the mural of the King at court survives –
dim channel through which bowls of raspberries
were once conveyed.

Where were these berries picked? we ask, spooning
them into our far away, snow-driven
mouths. *Mexico, Chile.* And we know
some twelve-year-old, or younger, has gathered
them, forty pounds per hour, down the cool
morning vines, a carrier strapped
to the waist, hands reaching, palms up
to catch any falling ripeness – then,
each berry grasped lightly between thumb
and fingers, given a turn – no jerk

or pull – to loose it from the vine.

I rest my spoon, watch Ray savor
our favorite fruit out of season,
like this poem written sixteen years after his death –
his 66th birthday. His pleasure is a red mountain
he scoops the top out of, like a crownless
king. Pleasure that had to traverse
unseemly diminishments and near deaths
to find his lips and tongue and teeth
in New York City, some publisher
footing our bills, making it
the sweeter, berries so red they are nearly
black, like that variety we never
got to sample: *Black Beauty*, said to be
"excellent and ever bearing." Like you.

A long way from Clatskanie
to this posh place! Our raw beginnings:
from the logging camps of the Olympic Peninsula or
yours in Yakima, the only house on the block with
an outhouse. No car so you walked everywhere,
your father filing saws at Boise Cascade, you
working the green chain like my brothers
in our mill town across state.

No wonder you can taste every one
of the 75 to 85 *druplets* in one
raspberry crown. If I were to tell you

these berries had escaped *root weevil, two-spotted
tortrix, cane maggot, spur blight, gray mold*, and even
a wart-like growth: *crown gall* – from bacteria
entering the plant through a wound – you
would just take the next bite
and say, *I believe it*.

One of the great things about living
longer, you said once, was *getting to learn more
of the story*. The details left by the visitor
to your grave, how a man's ashes were
stolen in an urn, along with a white Cadillac
convertible. The powdery remains jostled along
in the back seat with joyriders. The car
then torched so the ashes had to pass again
through fire, and twice refined, washed downstream,
the car nosed by then into a river.
Or maybe we retell it
so the ashes are still riding around
in that stolen car, coaching life's desperados.
In any case, the top is down, under
a cargo of stars.

Now you're talking, Ray says – delight
and the story going on into
the imperishable *now* of the never-again
raspberries he is consigning to his
one-and-only body beside me in that expansive,
gone – forever King Cole Bar.

Who said: *Raspberries do not keep
or travel well?* I'll stake my lot
with those ancient seafaring Chinese
who believed trees shed blood, or that to eat
the fruit of the 10,000 foot high Cassia tree
would make them immortal.

John Goodby

THE UNCLES

Uncles, talking the camshaft or the gimbal connected
to a slowly oscillating crank. The Uncles Brickell,
Swarfega kings, enseamed with swarf and scobs, skin
measled with gunmetal but glistening faintly, loud
in the smoke. Lithe and wiry above the lathe, milling out
a cylinder to a given bore. Uncles, pencil-stubs at their ears,
spurning ink, crossing sevens like émigré intellectuals,
measuring in thous and thirty-secondths (scrawled
on torn fag-packets); feinting with slide rules, racing,
but mild not as mild steel. Pockets congested, always. Uncles
with dockets for jobs, corners transparent with grease,
with a light machine oil. Time-served, my Uncles, branch-
ing out into doorhandles, grub-screws and the brass bits
that hold the front of the motor case to the rear flange
of the mounting panel. Release tab. Slightly hard of hearing
now, the Uncles, from the din of the shop, slowly nodding.
Uncles in 'Red Square'; uncles swapping tolerance gauges,
allan keys, telephone numbers, deals and rank commun-
ism. Forefingers describing arcs and cutting angles. White
and milky with coolants and lubricants, mess of order. Never
forgetting to ply a broom after. The missing half-finger, not
really missed any longer, just a banjo-hand gone west. My
Uncles still making a go of mower blades, on the road
at their age; offering cigars at Christmas. Uncanny if
encountered in visors, overalls, confounding nephews
in dignity of their calling, their epoch-stewed tea. Stand
a spoon in all their chamfered years, cut short or long. Uncles
immortal in the welding shed, under neon, lounge
as the vast doors slide to a cool blue desk. My Uncles.

Dana Goodyear

COUNTY LINE ROAD

Who was Father – a bandage, a mustache,
from time to time a saddening salt-and-pepper beard.
Mother? Some sort of monger – I see her with a pink fish,
my bodyweight, dill hairs clinging to her hands.
"Daddy is tired," I am said to have said,
and then I'd sing to him, sleeping.
He was an athlete, dislocated. He said, Forget Me Not.
Mother was never in the same room with any of us.
I think she was a hostess, in which case I should say,
Thank you for having me.

Ann Gray

YOUR BODY

I identified your face
and when he said is this, and gave your full name,
it wasn't enough to say, yes, he said I had to say,
this is, and give your full name.
It seemed to be all about names, but I only saw your face,
I wanted to rip back the sheet and say, yes this is his chest,
his belly, these are his balls and this the curve of his buttock.
I could have identified your feet, the moons on your nails,
the perfect squash ball of a bruise on your back,
the soft curl of your penis when it sleeps against your thigh.
I wanted to lay my head against your chest, to take your hands,
hold them to my face, but I was afraid your broken arm was
        hurting.
My fingers fumbled at your shirt but the makeshift sling had
        trapped it.
Your shirt, your crisp white shirt. The shirt I'd ironed on Friday.
The shirt that grazed my face when you leaned across our bed
to say goodbye. I watched the place where your neck
joins the power of your chest and thought about my head there.
He offered me your clothes. I refused to take your clothes,
Days later I wanted all your clothes. I didn't know what I
        wanted,
standing there beside you, asking if I could touch you,
my hands on your cheek. He offered me a lock of your hair.
I took the scissors. I had my fingers in your hair,
I could taste the black silken hair of your sex.
I wanted to wail all the Songs of Solomon,
I wanted to throw myself the length of you and wail.
I wanted to lay my face against your cheek.
I wanted to take the blood from your temple with my tongue,
I wanted to stay beside you till you woke.
I wanted to gather you up in some impossible way
to take you from this white and sterile place to somewhere

where we could lie and talk of love.
I wanted to tear off my clothes, hold myself against you.
He said, *take as long as you want*, but he watched me
through a window and everything I wanted seemed
undignified and hopeless, so I told him we could go,
we could leave, and I left you
lying on the narrow bed, your arm tied in its sling,
purple deepening the sockets of your eyes.

Geoffrey Hill

CITATIONS I

This not quite knowing what the earth requires:
earthiness, earthliness, or things ethereal;
whether spiritus mundi notices bad faith
or if it cares; defraudings at the source,
the bare usury of the species. In the end
one is as broken as the vows and tatters,
petitions with blood on them, the charred prayers
spiralling godwards on intense thermals.

No decent modicum, agreed. I'd claim
the actual is at once cruder and finer,
without fuss carrying its own weight. Still
I think of poetry as it was said
of Alanbrooke's war diary: a work done
to gain, or regain, *possession of himself,*
as *a means of survival* and, in that sense,
a mode of moral life.

Jane Hirshfield

SKY: AN ASSAY

A hawk flies through it, carrying
a still-twisting snake twice the length of its body.

Radiation, smoke, mosquitoes, the music of Mahler fly through it.

The sky makes room, adjusting its airy shoulders.

Sky doesn't age or remember,
carries neither grudges nor hope.
Every morning is new as the last one, uncreased
as the not quite imaginable first.

From the fate of thunderstorms, hailstorms, fog,
sky learns no lesson,
leaping through any window as soon as it's raised.

In speech, furious or tender,
it's still of passing sky the words are formed.
Whatever sky proposes is out in the open.

Clear even when not,
sky offers no model, no mirror – cloudy or bright –
to the ordinary heart: which is secretive,
rackety, domestic, harboring a wild uninterest in sky's disinterest.

And so we look right past sky, by it, through it,
to what also is moody and alters –
erosive mountains, eclipsable moons, stars distant but death-bound.

Judy Kendall

He threw a brick through the window
I double-glazed it

He picked the lock and made off with the computer
I took the chance to upgrade both

He took the car
I took up walking

He used a jemmy to break down the door
And take my tools, my iron, the upgraded computer and my
    aunt's antique mirror

The insurance came visiting
I wore a suit

I bought more expensive tools, irons and computers
Though I could not buy back my aunt's antique mirror

The police have padlocked the door back on its frame
And I am having a new one made of hardest mahogany

Next time he will respect the thickness of the door
That, at least, will be impregnable

Even if he carves it out, complete with frame,
And empties the whole house

Nick Laird

Use of Spies

Upright and sleepless,
having watched three bad movies,
I am flying across the ocean to see you.

I am a warrior and nothing will stop me,
although in the event both passport control
and a stoned cabbie from Haiti will give it a go,

but I meant to mention something else.

Just before dinner I woke in mid-air,
opened the shutter and saw the sun rising.
Light swung over the clouds like a boom.

The way it broke continually from blue
to white was beautiful, like some fabled
giant wave that people travel years to catch.

I thought I'll have to try and tell you that.

Jenny Lewis

INANA

he fathered her
then left a void

planted a seed
in the dark but the womb
grew darker

his absence
a poison that ran
down the walls

like damp

seven times seven
she shed herself

arched backwards
hung from a hook
through her belly button

a flower of muscle
peeled from the entry point

and round the tip
a flesh cushion
covered in scales
to hide the wires

in a rush
she entered the light
eyes polished wet

leaped upstream
the hook embedded still:
unseen

Tim Liardet

From NORTH OF EVERYTHING

for the Chinese cocklepickers drowned in February 2004

The throat at such a distance from the snarling man [...]
William Golding, *Pincher Martin*

I

They go down again, imagine them, spun
in a roaring vortex of gravel, spun

and somersaulted by the force of water,
burning water, bursting in the mouth like gases

or a storm of stones. The throat flung clear
and detached in the depths from each snarling man

is the throat that gulps. They are bound to each other,
all twenty-one, by whatever part of the body

touches at any given second, like a system of branches
struggling in and out – trying to climb –

what might be thought of as a trunk of light.
And they are bucked and thrown about, gulping

at water like buckled tin. They shed coins,
a Wellington boot, their eyes shrink back

into their heads, as if their lips are magnified;
until they are overtaken, overtaken

and the last lit up cellphone spins
to the bottom, spelling out: no network coverage.

Joanne Limburg

The Fall

Days old and when you wake you scream
for you wake to the knowledge of terrible things:
you were dragged unwilling to violent light and clanging noise
you are naked
your skin has been outraged with needles
baldness and myopia are your cradle gifts
cursed is the breast for your sake, therefore you toil for your
    nourishment
when you get home your mother heaven help her will weep and cry
    He hates me!
your father heaven help him will despairing change you for the
    third time one night and meet your shrieks with *Put a sock in it!*
your mother her body turning on itself will creep cold-blooded
    through your first five months and no one will know why
your arms will countless times be forced into sleeves and then
    throughbuggy straps
countless times you will wake at night in the dark alone and wonder
    Will they ever come for me again?
one day out shopping you will let go your mother's hand and find
    yourself lost in a forest of grown-up legs for seconds you
    will always remember as hours
at least one teacher will nurse for you an inexplicable hatred
two months ago your bully was born
the door to your college room will shut behind your parents you will
    look at the void on the face of the walls and feel yourself
    forsaken
more than once you will humiliate yourself thinking *This is love!* realise
    your mistake and have to avoid a certain street for evermore
there will be woeful attempts to breach the walls of well-dressed
    social citadels which will be met with misted eyes and
    tossed aside *Oh really?*s
for years you will work the dust turning up thorns and thistles
    eating your bread in the sweat of your face

you will come to inherit a world of botched repairs of hand-me-down
     guilt and poisoned privilege
you will have to answer for everything
you will forget what you know have to learn it all again and sit exams
for you have fallen from perfection like an idea into bungled execution
it is all my fault forgive me

John McAuliffe

Town

We leave tomorrow and the night finds me – where else –
down by the river, its current quiet and regular as a pulse,
silvery dark where the banked trees grow around
the outflow pipes. A bird takes off and goes to ground
in a commuter's site whose unpainted cement
is either half-finished or half-dismantled.
Farther off I see, bright as an oil rig, the Co-op shine
and foam, humming its bottom line.

The town's lit up, but no one comes back to reminisce,
intent as some evangelist smashing fossils,
making a religion out of feeling homesick...
Empty river, indifferent night: no joke.
We'll leave, grow older, return, say, 'Then what?'
On it all the glowing river twists the ground shut.

Mary MacRae

JURY

I'd noticed her hands before, large and quiet
in her lap as she listened through all the words
for the sound she wanted, the call from her scrap
of daughter, fed on demand
while we waited

and I thought of how she'd hold that feather-weight
in one hand while the other cupped the warm head
with its beating fontanelle close to her breast
as if that soft suck and tug
were all the world

and she could forget the knife, (one of a set),
with the serrated edge we'd seen already,
an ordinary kitchen knife, its ten-inch blade
nestling securely inside
a cling-wrapped box.

But it was the photo made me cry – her hand,
in colour, the palm flat for the camera,
fingers stretched apart to show the base of each
cut to the bone, ragged wounds
only half healed:

how painful it must have been to open out
the sheltering fist, uncurl her fingers and feel
the tight scabs crack, exposed for an indifferent
photographer to record
the naked truth.

And the moment all the others led up to
and away from – the moment before her hand
lost its grip on a handle made slippery with
his blood, slid down the blade? – that,
we couldn't see.

Allison McVety

PORTRAIT

My father carried his mother through Yugoslavia
and Greece. Stitched into the lining of his coat

and against regulations, she kept him company
through the days he hid in back rooms and under stairs;

suckled him on nights huddled in churchyards,
with only the chatter of his pad and key. He folded her

into his wallet, where she was rubbed by the grub of pound
notes, discharge papers, a thank-you letter

from General Tito. Around her neck, in miniature,
her brother, on a row of cultured pearls: his face

crimped by the crease of leather. His eyes show no hint
of my mother, though he has her lips. He is his pre-gassed,

pre-shot self. And I am the daughter of cousins, a woman
with no children. I think of losing her in a crowd, slipping her

into someone's jacket, an open bag, that sagging pocket
on the train, for her to live another life, our line travelling on.

Sarah Maguire

THE WATER DIVINER

Under the last shade of the pine trees
they wait together in silence
while he roams their wasted land –
a sleepwalker, driven, entranced.
Heat summons up dust devils
from the parched floor of the valley,
banners of sand unrolling in the breeze.

Who could remember water
in the face of this cracked earth –
scarred by dark fissures,
a hard web of desiccation
transfixed by the skulls of dry gourds
sprawling hollowed where they fell,
by the scorched hulls of fruit trees,
by the scratched evidence of grass?

Beneath soil turned to dust,
beneath the implacable bedrock,
he knows sweetness courses.
Pliancy babbling in darkness,
a wet ore threading through
potholes and boulders,
an aquifer swollen and cool.

His indigo robes seek out
their element, his wandering path
mimics a river in spate
chancing a new route to flood.
He balances the sappy twig
of precious hazelwood,
a hair-trigger sprung wetly green
under the peeled-back bark.

A slim boy in blue measuring a wasteland,
as if his feet could mend the torn soil
he walks the dried grid of the land,
conjuring liquid, his murmured prayers
big raindrops kicking up dust,
wanting an echo. But the level
branch holds as he paces the distance.

Dusk is coming. Then suddenly –
the sapling spasms and tears
from his grasp, and the water-diviner
faints where he stands. And now
he is a door opened on wetness.
He is a full well plumbed deep
underground. He is fodder for cattle.
An orchard in bloom.

Kathy Miles

A London Tale

How he loved those muted places
where fog sipped at his coat, and cold
nuzzled his cheek. He knew the old
familiar roads. Goulston Street, Bucks Row,
where wheels were muzzled by the smog,
the hiss of lamps in gilt burners,
their buttery circles of light.

He sauntered past the coffee houses,
rows of costermongers' stalls,
shops of linen and cigars. Here were markets
where women wrangled for bargains.
Piles of cake and fried fish, flowers, soaps and rice.
Barrows of mutton and oysters, tressel boards
heaped high with herring and spices.

How long he would wait here in the rain.
Pressed back against the brick, lighting
his pipe, he breathed in the smoke
of an early Whitechapel night.
He was the kind of man that nobody saw.
His cloak splashed by passing horses,
his hair sheened black with the spray.

He saw the factory girls, giggling on the way home,
huddled in sprigged shawls, shoes clipping
on the cobbles. He watched the seamstress
and maid, laundry woman and pastry cook.
Janet McDonald the Mangle Keeper,
Mrs Kidd the Ale Wife, who gave a curt nod,
her young son scurrying at her side.

He watched the potboys whistling to the taverns,
saw the whores slump at street corners.
He imagined them going back to sugared tea,
a warm fire. Peeling off bodice and chemise,
their stockings held with garters.
Such white legs, skin glimmering in candlelight
hair pulled from pins, tumbling to slim waists.

And still he waited. Past the time when men spilled
from taverns and saloons, full of port-wine
and honey-gin, and girls from the chorus
poured from the door of the Lyric or Savoy.
Spruce clerks hurried home.
Doctors on call hastened from their beds,
their watch chains gravely swinging.

A small man, one you wouldn't notice.
Dapper in his button-boots and gaiters.
A dark felt hat turned down, a horse-shoe pin,
his cuffs and collars trimmed with astrakhan.
He strolls from the shadows. She turns a weary smile.
'Good evening, sir. My name? It's Catherine Eddowes'.

David Morley

FICTION

I was haunted by falsehood from the start, some brink of this reached
by late childhood. To keep lying, to pile it up, was how to live
because fiction tied the parts and parcels of name. Fiction was the poached
life history of travelling folk. Fiction was the electricity and rates.
Paid for your shoes. Fiction took the bus to the store, was allowed
by family law to shoplift. Fiction told the old story every night.
Fiction was poor but dishonest. Fiction gave birth before a grate,
placed my placenta on the sizzling clinkers. Fiction liked comforts.
She had the brains to earn them, but Fiction stayed out late.
Fiction was a virgin before marriage, of course. She laid the hoard
of the tale tall before you. You were bidden to believe in this
despite the fact it was fiction. You had to grow askew. It's hard
quarrelling with Fiction. Because Fiction is you: your bones
are thin beams of fable; and your blood, when it pouts at your lips
draws through its black alley. Fiction has good fingers, she has sewn
then unstitched the same shroud for years. Fiction longs for reunion
with her lover. He died strong and striking. He swam out of turn
down a long and burning sea of blood. Fiction yearned to restring the yarn
for herself, demanded a better ending. Her children learned their part
and played it from affection. But Fiction began to believe her tale.
                                    It collapsed into art
in which Fiction was the lead, and her children chapters and verses.
Her friends would spin about her screaming *Author, Author.*
Haunted by so much falsehood, a brink was reached.

Sharon Morris

FOR THE FIG TREE

At first, it was the hummingbird
that gave the fig tree meaning.

We would wait at the window
for the humming bird to appear –
enamel green, a flash of iridescent pink
on its neck (a dare or revelation)
hovering horizontal, wings a blur,
its bill deep in the base of a leaf,
only a faint hum in the world
from this, the smallest bird
in North America,
the only bird to fly backwards...

You pick up the poems of Rilke
and let it fall to this page –
Fig tree,
for how long have I found meaning
in the way you almost skip the flowering
and thrust your pure mystery
unsung, into the early set fruit...

It's the fig tree we wake to, leaves
pressed against the window pane;
it's the fig tree, which shields us,
saves us from each other's threshold,
from exposure, from shame:

I don't want you to miss the light,
light suffused with ocean-mist
that eases the distance to Marin
and the east bay.
There could be a wider view from here...

...But we hang back,
ah, we revel in the flowering, and enter
the belated inner space
of our ultimate fruit already betrayed.

The day the branches were pruned,
carelessly, the stubs left open to the sky,
a new cold light stepped
into the room –
now the season of its fruit is over
a pinch of sea opens
with the fall of each separate leaf.

Graham Mort

ADVERTISING EXECUTIVE WITH SPARROWHAWK

This morning the lane was laced with frost,
its glow of leaves curled brandy snaps
falling from the trees.

Clouds, black and gilt-edged. A headful of
Scotch. St. Vitus hands, the thought of
office treachery uppermost.

Dawn's crucible melting the slag of night, the
Saab retching to the road towards another
day of innuendo and damned lies.

Then the sparrowhawk straddling a dove
ambushed from the blackthorn hedge –
one moment coasting the wind

towards all that's ripe and good in life,
the next shafted by some grey-backed
bastard gliding up behind.

The dove lay scuttled, oozing its jewellery
of blood, the hawk glared at me – mere
meat – and only just too big to take.

I thought of how the meek are clutched
by death, the way the hawk felt nothing
good for any living thing, then

how it strutted, stared, flew up quiet as
smoke, chest barred with rage, its eyes
so hard they dented mine.

I changed gear, watched the moon trying
to haunt the day; the engine warm
and purling, needles on the

fascia taut, the car wheels humming
past a badger's mess of spilled-up
guts. Another day. I'll tick it off

tonight, drinking to forget slogans and
video spools and younger, smarter men.
All that seemed so real until then –

that moment of the dove's scattered life,
the hawk staking its claim before crows in
dark suits did their job of aftercare.

But maybe I'll remember how this copse I
drive by every day was melting in the sun;
how I stopped to smoke and sat

here, outside words; watched mist dripping
from the trees, imagined how this hush
must always be here, like the birds.

Paul Muldoon

SOCCER MOMS

They remember Gene Chandler topping the charts with
    "Duke of Earl"
when the boys were set on taking the milk bar's one banquette
and winning their hearts, Mavis and Merle,

as it seemed their hearts might be first to yield,
hearts before minds. Time for stilettos. Time for spivs with shivs.
The time of day when light fails on the field

while their daughters, themselves now tweenie girls,
crowd round a coach for one last tête-à-tête.
They remember Gene Chandler topping the charts with
    "Duke of Earl"

while the world still reeled
from the anti-Castro Cubans going to sea in a sieve,
as it seemed. Their hearts might be first to yield

if only after forty years of one plain, one purl,
on the sweater they've sweated over for a Bay of Pigs vet,
and winning their hearts, Mavis and Merle,

may now be faintly likelier for a well-heeled
schlub to whom they once wouldn't so much as give
the time of day. When light fails on the field

a schlubster linesman will unfurl
an offside flag that signals some vague threat,
they remember. Gene Chandler topping the charts with
    "Duke of Earl"

for three weeks only in 1962 might have taught them to shield
themselves against the lives their daughters briefly relive,
as it seemed *their* hearts might be first to yield

to this free kick that forever curls
past the goal-mouth, a ball at once winging into the back of the net
and winning. Their hearts, Mavis and Merle,

hanker for the time when it was not yet revealed
failure's no less literal than figurative,
the time of day when light fails on the field

and gives back a sky more muddy than mother-of-pearl,
so it's with a deepening sense of regret
they remember Gene Chandler topping the charts with
     "Duke of Earl"
and winning their hearts, Mavis and Merle.

Michael O'Siadhail

Never to forget the towering dreams
Of heaven-hankers before their time,
Brick for stone, for mortar slime

So many offered for madcap schemes.
Over and again some other fable
Of perfection: *Let us make us a name.*

Another skyscraper and still the same.
Fall and fall all spires of Babel
To lovely confusions of our gabble

Scattered abroad on the face of the earth
As slowly we relearn each other's worth,
Difference and sameness incommensurable.

In all our babble birds of a feather –
Aithníonn ciaróg ciaróg eile,
Beetle knows beetle – *Qui se ressemble*

S'assemble – all over flock together,
Skeins of hope, *gleich und gleich...*
Like to like, kind calls fellow –

Rui wa tomo o yobu in Tokyo.
Around our globe a netted Reich,
Of random trust, cross-ties of civility,

Farflung jumbles of non-violent voices
Argue our intertwining choices
To weave one planet's fragile city.

Marita Over

SPIDERS

A Rorschach inkblot is
fastened on the porcelain.
Will not respond at first, nor wash away.
Does not thin. Does not appear

to bloom into a colour chart
like those ink chromatograms
whose wet throats bleed the secrets of their
blackest composition.

It is an alert black hand
around my heart, squeezing it dry.
This is a stain that stays.
No lady can easily wash it away.

Yet all through October
the creature thrived on our lavender.
Females fattened
gently in their spinnings.

Soft flesh, speckled
like mute thrushes,
or sun-warmed miniature toads
intent on digestion.

And our garden all autumn
like a good sleep you wake from
the threads to your hinterland cut and forgotten,
contained them out of sight and mind.

November now though, with both taps on,
the gushing lifts her too light body

on a swirl that spins her
drifting towards the plug-hole.

There she staggers, little hag,
on a penny-pinching stint,
making thrifty
silk of the water.

Sandeep Parmar

The Octagonal Tower

History is the love that enters us through death; its discipline is grief.
Anne Michaels

I

Whatever rage has come through these sealed doors,
And scalded us black and frayed, we have no name for.
We cannot explain the quiet, sleepless shift of whispers,
A procession of shrouds along our corridors,
Or the diverted eyes that cloud to see a row of winter oaks outside
Shocked in their dendritic fizz. And if we do know it,
It is in the blood, in this terrible synapse of sky, in the road away.
From our house we drive down through a sunken valley
Where, like a crypt, it is forever the hour of the dead.

You have always worn the wheel, pushed your hands and wrists
Through its axes, as though it were a shackle. Driven, hunched.
It is the same – the sting of yucca and eucalyptus, a vein of pink
Bougainvillea purged in hot pulses off roof tops – a fragrant
    massacre –
And the same steady road you drive every time afraid to speak,
Afraid to ask when I will leave you alone in that house with your wife.
I translate your favourite song in my mind: *This song of mine, no one*
    will sing.
This song of mine that I sing myself will die tomorrow with me.

An October night, 1975. A sudden rain has liquefied the earth.
Mud isn't enough. There is a word you use that means more than
    mud,
It is the sound of a foot, sunken to the ankle, pulling itself out –
The awful suck of uprooting. Like a scream, it is the fear of standing
So long that you might stay and sink forever. This sound trails
Behind you and your brother as you walk the fields one last time.

You will leave and not return for ten years, to marry my mother
Who you've not yet met. Your four bare feet make an agreement
    with the earth
To remember. The earth prints its own response in your shadows.

II

Holidays are uncertain times. The marble face of an old king's grief
Deflects the spectacle of his queen's death in each perfect tessera.
The Taj rises above the Jammuna, doubles paradise in the mastery
    of slaves.

Holidays are uncertain times; their hands are cut off of arms
    thrown up
In celebration. Now they too mourn, and skyward pray to
    phantom limbs
In the gardens of heaven, alone to pluck and preen.

They are carted away without ceremony, along with the remains
    of stone
that, like teeth, fall out of swooning heads. The funeral begins.
Mumtaz, hollow as a bride, is veiled in by her white, carved lid.

No one knows when you were born. They think it was an Autumn
    month.
At five you asked where your mother was. Your false soot lashes
    pooled with fear.
Gone to your grandmother's. Later you found her picture.
A woman propped up, freshly dead, her hands emptied of the past.
And you, seated on her lap, two years old, holding her
And what held her forever in that exposure.

III

The road widens just past tracts of arched houses; you drive faster
    and grip the wheel.
I say I won't leave till after the New Year, but by now it doesn't
    matter.

138

Your knuckles are bloodless, and your stoic eyes are the calm
    surface of a timepiece.

Shah Jehan, imprisoned in a tower by his son, was sent a gold platter
The day of the coup with the head of his chosen heir upon it.
Seeing this the old king fell, knocked the teeth out of his head.
For eight years he watched the Taj from his window, from across
    the river,
In a diamond mounted in the wall that reflected it a million times
    over.
The soft marble hands of his wife extended to him, to the empty
    casket beside her.
When the river filled, he walked across it.

When the door opens, only one of us leaves. I watch your car until
    it is far down
Through the shadows of trees. The road receives you, and the house
    receives you,
As does the galley of water, the trimmed hedge, the cold, sterile cell.

In your wallet, you carry a picture of my mother, from before my
    birth,
When she was only yours. Her pinks match the pinks of flowers;
She bows her head into the branch and smiles, as beautiful as a
    queen.
Love is incidental, time-bound. Pain is eternal, is locked to it by
    memory.
It is the memory of love we love. It is the memory that fattens on
    pain –
Of these small deaths and these stone walls. The crown that has
    sunken
From your ears and hangs around your neck is all that remains.

Mario Petrucci

Night Flaw

Hard-down on your street it squats – each
smash of light, the thunderous grab right
on its heels with hardly time to count to
One – tonight autumn breaks her back
across your eaves, shudders panes as with
fingers laced to one strange hand we part
nets on a world – freed of intentions,
its canopy grazing your backboned semis,
that burn of photocopiers splicing air as air
grows thick and resinous, chill as cream
on skin, spilling in at your open sash from
sky's orange-pink cornea whose capillaries
run quick pulses of electric blood
        – seized, possessed
of so much witness.

Jacob Polley

THE OWLS

I hear the owls in the dark yews
behind the house – children out late
or lost, their voices worn away.
They've forgotten their names and wait

to be called again by mothers
who miss them, so they might return
with fingers and human faces.
But their sadness, too, is long gone.

Their voices are as empty
and unlovable as glass
and no one calls into the trees.

Little gods, they've forsaken us
as we have them! They sit and cry,
glorified, and couldn't care less.

Maurice Riordan

From THE IDYLLS

'We're more or less standing on the water table.'

The men were in the Bog waist deep in muddy ground.
They were cutting a drain from the pond to the stream. The
hope was to free up land for pasture and my father was
following instructions from the Department Engineer. 'You
could say the water is meant to run from head to toe, while
the people go east and west across it.'

'In former times,' he explained, 'an old road came through
the farm and exited via Keegan's Passage onto the Pound
Road, then away towards the city. By day and even at night
there was a traffic of carts and people driving animals, of
men on horseback, tinkers, hawkers, constabulary. All sorts,
who might stop at the pump for talk and refreshment.'

'Were there no rogues and thieves in those days?' asked
Davey Divine.

'A duck or a rabbit might go missing but never anything
of value.'

'Though the road's no longer in use there are still those
who know,' said Moss. 'Tramps and trappers and suchlike.
They hold onto things longer than most. And they remember
the paths and where the stepping stones are.'

'So that's how you'd find Carney the Knacker or Snook
Buckley asleep beside you on a cold morning.'

'If it's beside you he'd be, 'Son. But you were saying about
the water?'

'Well, in Alice Warren's time they diverted the water to
create a lake.'

'What was a lake for?'

'God only knows,' Moss said. 'The Warrens were English.'

'Pleasure, I suppose.'

My father traced the course of the water along the south
side of the Paddock. There it looped around like a moat
outside the high stone walls of the yard. He pointed to the

hollow where the geese were grazing below the Lane Gate.

'You can see the brooklime's taken over and it's a softer green. That's where it was.'

By now the men had stopped their work. They had climbed out of the drain and were looking back across the rushes and furze bushes towards the farm yard, picturing what it must have been like.

'A lake,' said Davey at last. 'A pleasure lake.'

Neil Rollinson

WILDLIFE

You get addicted to the ink,
or the pain; one or the other.
When she came in here for that rose

on her shoulder, I might've known
it would come to this – years later,
her body painted from head

to foot in a thousand colours.
I read her now like a picture book,
a china vase, a dream of my own making.

I've pierced her ears, her nose,
put studs in her nipples,
a silver ring through the hood

of her clitoris. I've covered
her breasts with moths,
her thighs with dolphins.

Her back is a forest of shrubs
and birds, her arms are vines,
her belly a nest of vipers.

I've touched her where only
a lover should touch, have heard her sigh
in the cold November dusk

of my studio. I've felt her burn,
at the brush of a finger, and hardly
a word passed between us.

I think of her sometimes lying
in bed, the buzz of my needle
still in her skin, a lover

tracing the braille of a new tattoo,
or him holding her, gently,
amazed at the wildlife swarming

under his hands, how she moves
in the flicker of candles; or watching
her sleep, how he loses himself

in the richness and distance.
The journeys he takes.
The stories he finds in her skin.

Suzanna Roxman

WELCOME TO ELSINORE

On the ramparts here you won't meet your father
or even mother, only some fisherman
carrying herring, dead in a basket.

It's October with lacquered wild rosehips,
perfectly edible where sand and meadow touch,
tended without poison which nobody needs.

You won't see that well behaved family girl,
curtseying and obedient, questioning little,
in a pink dress till she dissolves in mud.

But drowning remains perfectly possible.
Moats convey swans from another story
and surrealism yields black shiny divers

emerging among diverse wreaths of seaweed.
At the Sounds edge anoraked anglers freeze,
each line yearning south.   Sit down

on shingle while sunshine lingers by the castle
backdrop, verdigris elongated whorled
pointed seashells for fairytale turrets.

This wind confuses you, this coast without passion,
no Shakespearean dangerous crags.
You began here once but decided not to stay.

Fiona Sampson

World Asleep

Darkness opens like a gate
again. My fingers on your latch
are tender when they lift the tongue,
slip a catch, then hesitate

across the entrance where you wait.
Your smile's a darkness joined to dark:
it widens as I close this gap –
almost noiseless. It's getting late:

nocturnal landscape – a country
I didn't choose – and I'm alone with you.
I kiss the soil. Its sweet reek
of straw's like longing, a snare of honey

to bite and bring me home to you:
a costly *heimat*. A world, asleep.

Michael Schmidt

The teddy bear cholla and the fat fat

*

Oh buckthorn, devil, whipple, teddy bear

*

Oh beavertail, oh pancake, porcupine

*

Oh plump saguaro with your hairy arms, I love
Each of you with a different nerve of heart.
Especially you, so trim, so pert, your birds
Cupped in your pits and crotches, little friends

*

Oh areoles and aureoles, the orioles
With yellow caps are havering and hot
Making themselves a breeze with their cut wings

*

I ask the docent and he indicates

*

Oh nation, how you might have been, spread from
So sure an order, with such tendering love

Seni Seneviratne

THE ORPHAN DOLL

My mother always told me *Hold your sister's hand*
and hurry home from school, don't linger.
But on that day in nineteen fifty-six, the broken house
next to the four-a-penny sweet shop made us stop.
It smelled of *Don't go in there*, held us helpless in its
rotted doorway, sherbet lemon fizzing on our tongues.

I saw her then, the orphan doll, abandoned in the dust
between the damaged floorboards. Her blue eyes stared
right into my soul, set off a flock of birds inside my head
(so I couldn't hear my mother's *Hurry home from school*),
made me linger, wriggled my fingers free, pulled me
from my sister's grasp towards her waiting eyes.

I almost reached her, almost saved her from the dust
and smell. But my sister, fuelled by her duties,
cautioned by the certainty of blame,
caught the hem of my coat and dragged me back so hard
I fell and all the four-a-penny sweets went rolling
from my pockets down the street, like guilty secrets.

Saradha Soobrayen

MY CONQUEROR

She circles me with her Portuguese compass
and settles just long enough to quench her thirst.
She discards my Arabian name *Dina Arobi*,
and calls me *Cerné*, from island of the swans.

With the hunger of a thousand Dutch sailors
and a tongue as rough as a sea biscuit she stakes
a longer claim and makes herself comfy,
bringing her own Javanese deer, pigs and chickens.

Defending her lust for breasts and thighs, she blames
the ship's rats for sucking the Dodo from its shell.
Looking past my ebony limbs, she sees carved boxes
and *marron* hands at work stripping my forests.

She renames me in honour of Prince Maurice
of Nassau. A good choice, sure to scare off pirates
keen to catch a bite of river shrimp, flamed in rum.
Disheartened by cyclones and rat bites, she departs.

For eleven years, I belong to no one. I sleep
to the purring of turtledoves. Sheltered by a circle
of coral reef, my oval shape rises
from the coast up to the peaks of mountains.

A westerly wind carries her back. She unbuttons
her blue naval jacket slowly and takes me.
I am her *Île de France*, her *petit pain*.
She brings spaniels. She captures *marrons*

who are pinned down and flogged, each time they run.
She takes her fill in Port Louis, shipping casks
of pure sweetness to the tea-drinking ladies of Europe.

Young Baudelaire jumps ship on his way to India.

His step-father wants to cure him of 'literature'.
Once a poet makes his mark, no tide can wash away
his words: *'Au pays parfumé que le soleil caresse'*.
And what can I say, he was so delicious!

Sadly sweet Baudelaire soon finds himself
in such a profound melancholy,
after seeing a whipping in the main square,
after two weeks, he sails to France, leaving me

a sonnet. With the pride and jealousy of
the British Admiralty she punishes me
with her passion for corsets, sea-blockades
and endless petticoats wide as the Empire.

The oldest profession is alive and thrives
in my harbours; strumpets and exports, cross-
dressing captains and girls in white breeches.
Boys who like boys who like collars and chains.

She brings a pantomime cast of *malabars*
and *lascars* to my shores. Their passage back
to India guaranteed, if only they can read the scripts.
The cane breaks backs. Tamil, Urdu, Hindi, cling

to their skins like beads of sweat. Hundreds of tongues
parched like the mouths of sweet-hearts in an arranged
ceremony. She is kind and ruthless and insists
on the Queen's English. At night Creole verve slips in

and makes mischief. Each time she comes she pretends
it's the first time she has landed here, but she soon
becomes bored. Tired of flogging and kicking
the dogs. She doesn't know which uniform to wear.

'I'm no one and everyone', she complains.
'And you have no more distinguishing marks
left to conquer'. She pulls down her Union
Jack; it falls like a sari, around her bare feet.

Marrons: Creole name given to the slaves taken from Madagascar and transported convicts.
Malabars and *Lascars*: Hindu and Muslim indentured labourers.
These names are disparaging terms in Mauritian Creole.

Matthew Sweeney

The Race

Stavros blows the whistle,
the race is on –
the one-legged monkey
going like a piston
takes an early lead,
but watch that goose,
webbed feet flailing
beak pecking blood,
or over on the right,
the galloping donkey
with the blindfold on –
or surging through the middle
the snorting boar
with the cat on his back,
and at his shoulder,
the charging bear
with fluorescent fur,
but ostrich, the favourite
is limping to a halt,
and the leopard lies dead,
face in the dirt,
and the rabbit is hiding
in a palm tree.
And standing at the start,
howling his head off,
is the tied-up wolf.

Jeffrey Wainwright

CALL DEATH AN OBSERVATION (i)

call death an observation,
a supplied fact, ever more precisely noted
(mistakes have been made though, ask any Goth)
and some vital sign may still be missed –
a monitoring may be merely mechanical,
conducted dozily after lunch, or not adhere
to best practice –
but from the many instances
the law 'We Die' has been induced,
and if shaggy at first, improvised –
and may still be so compared with
what might be to come – is now deduced,
the maths showing us how much we can infer
of what we do not know

it seems irrefragable, and as long as the law
coincides with observation it holds

CALL DEATH AN OBSERVATION (ii)
if lines and circles are all our own work
have we invented death?
motionlessness seems to be
what was decided upon,
that she or he could no longer shift for herself
and would just dry there
or deliquesce depending,
although many (most?)
have traditionally not gone on such appearances
but when forced to give up say:
but this is not the real line,
what is real has no lines
because no space or time

because a line must be an act in time
and mind

because it is not bearable
to live with lines and circles

CALL DEATH AN OBSERVATION (iii)

mathematics makes up the bolus,
what could be truer than such proceedings?
the equations of fluids in and fluids out,
the charting and cross-checking
towards a line to be pronounced upon:
the baby-like milky regurge
at the corner of the mouth,
sent out, uncalibrated, bubbling slightly

but somewhere there the point –

it happens always and the line is true

*

and before the May-dawn, the conventional dream-ship,
bulk cargo freighter, or sharp-prowed liner
the black *Normandie* or another such,
seemingly unworked, eyeless, unhurried:
and knowing you cannot row aside

Susan Wicks

Man in a Blue Rain-cape

Here where windows dribble stains, the gutters
choked and sweating black-green,
he's in his element.
You watch him hop and flap
downhill, spreading his arms,
to wheel like a pigeon over plastic chairs
and tables; nylon feathers flutter in the wind

as he loops the loop and circles, looking for a spire
or ridge-tile where he can tuck his head
under his rainproof wing and dream
his blue migration dreams.
What can he possibly have said

in passing? What a very English bird
to fly in rain unfazed
and roost in hollow trees and wake
you in the morning with his inveterate singing.

Jackie Wills

Don't Commit Adultery

In a hotel room, rented flat, a friend's place, beach,
car, caravan, your own bed, his or her bed,
the children's beds, with dogs, that guy from the Red
House, your boss, on a motorbike, in a coach,

wearing that old leather jacket, after a cricket
match, in a tent, while your second child is being born,
watching a famous boxer doing press ups in the gym,
while your first child is being born, after 10 shots

of Greek brandy, with someone who writes fan mail,
with your therapist, the priest, manager or director,
wife of your best friend, while your wife is having a
hysterectomy, because she has thrush, piles,

with your son's teacher, when your husband's in a coma,
with your son's girlfriend, in the Pussycat Club, with a lap
dancer, while smoking a cigar or reading the latest crap
crime fiction, contemplating Escher's prints in the Alhambra,

while your partner's leaving a message on your mobile,
by e mail, live webcam, wearing stiletto heels, while your wife
is undergoing radiotherapy, while flying a plane, in Fife
station, with a doctor, over the baby listening device.

Tamar Yoseloff

Voyage

The train sails through field, docks in middle-
manager cities: Coventry, Milton Keynes,
the track before us a fact of our expansion,
the night inevitable – sick phosphorescence of lights
coming on, of platforms rushing past,
the names of towns illegible with speed,
their tower blocks blown back in a sudden squall.
On the page a man is drowning:
I only have to close the book to forget him.
He's history. The present is about the train
hurtling past on the opposite track, steering
for where I've just been; the flotsam of travel:
the paper cup, the empty miniature,
the folded tabloid. Old news. Salt on my tongue.

35133

POETRY REVIEW

founded in 1911 by Harold Monro

Britain's only world-class poetry magazine
includes:

- ❧ Poetry
- ❧ Essays
- ❧ Criticism
- ❧ Poetry news from Britain and
  around the world

THE POETRY SOCIETY

Orders: 020 7420 9881
www.poetryreview.org.uk
UK Annual Subscription: £30